Teaching Through Poetry
Writing and the drafting process

George Marsh

HODDER AND STOUGHTON
LONDON SYDNEY AUCKLAND TORONTO

For Teddy and Gwen

British Library Cataloguing in Publication Data
Marsh, George
    Teaching through poetry: writing and
    the drafting process.
    1. Poetry. Composition—For schools
    I. Title
    808.1
ISBN 0 340 42458 3

First published in Great Britain 1988

© 1988 George Marsh

Typeset in Linotron Plantin by Wessex Typesetters,
(Division of The Eastern Press Ltd),
Frome, Somerset
Printed and bound in Great Britain for
Hodder and Stoughton Educational,
a division of Hodder and Stoughton Ltd,
Mill Road, Dunton Green, Sevenoaks, Kent
by Page Bros (Norwich) Ltd, Norwich

Contents

Acknowledgments

The author and publishers would like to thank the following for permission to reproduce material in this book:

The Hokuseido Press, Tokyo for the haiku on pp. 106 and 107 from *Haiku* Volumes 3 and 4 translated by R. H. Blyth; Tabitha Tuckett for her poem on p. 127; City Lights Books, San Francisco for 'Breakfast' on p. 87 from *Paroles* translated by Lawrence Ferlinghetti; Penguin Books Ltd for the extracts from 'Chivvy' by Michael Rosen on p. 63 from *You Tell Me* by Roger McGough and Michael Rosen, and 'Death' on p. 62 from *Medieval English Verse* translated by Brian Stone; Faber and Faber Limited for the extract from 'The Naming of Cats' on p. 10 by T. S. Eliot from *Old Possum's Book of Practical Cats*; Laurence Pollinger Ltd and the Estate of Mrs Frieda Lawrence Ravagli for 'Peach' on p. 21 by D. H. Lawrence; London Publishing House Ltd/Warner Brothers Music Ltd for the extracts from 'Reasons to be Cheerful Part 3' on pp. 63 and 91 by Ian Dury; Lucien Stryk and the Estate of Takashi Ikemoto for the haiku on pp. 105, 106 and 107 from *The Penguin Book of Zen Poetry*; André Deutsch for 'Rondel' by Villon on p. 111 translated by Mervyn Savill; The English Centre for 'US Dreads' by Dave Martin on p. 26 from *City Lines: Poems by London School Students 1982*; Carcanet Press Ltd/New Directions Publishing Corp. for 'The Locust Tree in Flower' by William Carlos Williams on p. 22 from *Collected Poems, Volume I: 1909–1939*, copyright 1939; NAB/UGC for the extract on p. 27 from Strategy Document.

Preface

This book is intended for teachers in middle and secondary schools. The same principles apply from the junior classes up to teenagers, and poetry teaching is so inconsistent in English schools that whatever the age of the pupils you teach your new class is unlikely to have been taken through a developed writing programme before. At times, approaches suited especially to younger pupils or older ones are addressed, but in general the material is presented using examples of pupils' writing drawn from right across the age range, and it will be up to each teacher to judge what might be successful with his or her class.

Teachers who are not English specialists will find that explanations are full enough to give clear directions. One of the primary aims of the book is to give non-specialists the confidence to feel that this is a curriculum area that they can understand. Poetry teaching is not only for Masons initiated into the arcane mysteries of the ancient art, but for all. There are language-teaching principles to bear in mind; there are skills that the teacher can develop through practice; there are classroom activities and forms of organisation that have proved keys for releasing locked-up language; and by adopting the 'drafting' approach described here, teachers can systematically develop quality in their pupils' writing.

Poetry arouses fear and suspicion in many teachers, and children can sense these feelings. There are a number of damaging misconceptions that have to be negotiated before the way is clear, and these are the subject of the first chapter. Luckily, it is easy to put these right: the best way is simply to plunge in and show the pupils what the expressive medium can mean for them and, as their writing flows, the fears and misconceptions melt away behind them. Like most human activities that beginners fear they will never understand, poetry teaching turns out to be simpler once one is doing it.

I hope that English specialists will find that the discussion of poems by children, and of the development of writing skills, strengthens their sense of the value of their teaching, and renews their confidence to stand up for what their instincts tell them is right.

I would like to thank the children whose work is quoted here. It has not been possible to seek permission from them all to publish their work, but I acknowledge my debt to them. They were, or still are, at the following schools: Quinton-Kynaston Comprehensive School, ILEA; Knottingley High School, West Riding; Mayfield Comprehensive School, and Priory Secondary School, Portsmouth; Springfield Comprehensive School, Cosham, Hampshire; and Copnor Middle School, Corpus Christi Middle School, Crofton Hammond Junior School, Emsworth First School, Hart Plain First School, Hulbert Middle School, Langstone Middle School, Meadowlands Middle School, Meon Middle School, Northgate Middle School, Saint Paul's First and Middle School, and Saint Swithun's Middle School, all in Portsmouth or south-east Hampshire. I am also grateful to John Blanchard, Derek Giles, Ewan Proctor and Julie Scarborough, all teachers who have been responsible for some of the children's writing.

I have adopted the policy of presenting children's work correctly spelt and optimising the layout.

Dr Tony Callen, Bernard MacDonagh, Robert Miles, Fiona Wray and Andrew Steeds have each given me valuable advice on drafts of some of the chapters, and I appreciate their help. Ian Mills kindly took on some of my work to give me extra time to teach in schools.

I am very grateful for the support of my mother and father, who have helped me in every possible way, and of my two sons, who have left me uninterrupted while I wrote, and brought me cups of tea at regular intervals.

George Marsh
August 1988

PART ONE
The Rationale

1 Misconceptions: Nooligan in the Crystal Kingdom

If we say to pupils, 'Write a poem', what goes through their minds? What responses have been provoked by hitting the button 'poem'?

Some feel instant hostility – they know that poetry is part of an effeminate culture that people like them reject wholesale. A teacher asking them to take part in it compromises their dignity.

Others just feel hopelessly unable to relate to the task; poetry is a mystery way beyond their ken, for people from families that go to the theatre.

Amongst those who are prepared to have a go there are various peculiar notions of 'what a poem should be'. Most pupils are likely to approach it with a view to producing what they think the teacher wants, rather than perceiving what is intrinsically interesting in the task. The only way round this problem is to show them gradually that you have no special conception of what you want, other than that they should discover an interest in the task. In other words, it depends on building a relationship of trust: they learn that they do not have to perform tricks for you, write the poems for you that you yourself cannot write, or compete with Milton and Wordsworth. They learn that you are responsive to any really felt experience of their own and they can trust you as a reader with their confusion and their vulnerability.

Few teachers, however, *do* know what they like in poetry, and pupils often learn from the clues they are given that as long as they produce something vaguely resembling some odd conception of 'what a poem ought to look like', the teacher will be only too grateful. Therefore some pupils learn that endless acrostics, or anything that is dripping with kindly sentiment, or any galloping rhyme, or any description of a natural scene using a pretentious vocabulary and expressing vaguely exalted feelings will satisfy the demand for 'creative writing'. The baleful shadow of the old

O level literature syllabus is detectable here: that course was the last acquaintance many teachers had with the study of literature and, not surprisingly, they think poems are baffling ingenious museum pieces which we have a duty to respect and not mess with.

The rest of this chapter examines some of the most common misconceptions the teacher may encounter.

'Ideal' Poems

The following poems show how the pupil's notion of what a poem is may affect the writing. It is clear that Jean is pleasing her teacher by imitating (cleverly and successfully) her model of an ideal poem:

A WINTER DAY

Think of a cool wintry day
Snow twinkling in the sun like
Bright cheerful eyes or stars
Shining in a dark night sky.
Like crystals in a crystal Kingdom
Cool and clear.
Like water dripping from a tap and
Sunlight shining through like a rainbow.
Think of a cool wintry day.
Snow twinkling in the sun.

Jean (12)

Her vocabulary is taken from the drawer in the corner, never otherwise used, labelled 'Poetry': twinkling, crystal, cheerful, rainbow. The poem is a Christmas card vision of beauty, and consists of three elaborately extended similes for 'snow twinkling in the sun'. It seems that Jean has a facility with language and can do what she sets out to do. It is a shame, however, that what she sets herself to do is to reproduce a notion of a 'poem' as a weaving together of decorative similes in cut-glass language. If her teacher were to liberate her from this misconception she would discover poetry as a real communicative medium.

'Leopard', like 'A Winter Day', is taken from a school magazine and is a clever piece of writing. It is by an upper sixth former:

LEOPARD

The leopard
  ripples
    through the high grass.
  Hunched in motion
    streamlining
his bodywork;
  revving
    up.
  Startles
into life;
  fleeting gliding
  striping
    through the rustling
rippling
    long high grass.

Ian (17)

Ian has a much more up-to-date view of 'what a poem ought to look like' than Jean. In his case, it is one consistently developed extended metaphor with some striking technical effects. He has used a short line and hyperactive layout, which appropriately expresses movement, and a cumulative series of participles. Ian has used a bold, modern idea in comparing natural beauty with mechanical power. In the absence of any felt reality, however, this skill just looks flashy and self-regarding.

Contrast 'Leopard' with 'Methuselah' below, a poem about an old horse that was kept on wasteland. It was written by a CSE stream 14 year old, who had some serious literacy problems – the first draft was almost unreadable because the standard of spelling and handwriting was so poor.

METHUSELAH

Wise and Inquisitive cocked ears, with bold dark eyes,
  Nostrils quiver and his muzzle gently
  Seeks the sugar in my palm.

Urgent eye-lashes flicker, as the eyes watch
  A hundred places, for any forward movement
  I may intend.

He has seen his years, he has knowledge of dark shady places.
  He remembers the day he was set free,

He was no clock-work mouse,
He needn't return to be re-wound,
He was powerful, worthy of his women,
Barbarous, Intelligent, Spirited.

Alas – he was tamed, humbled, deprived of his freedom,
never to gain.
Yet he had comfort.
A shelter, water, food plenty, yet still
He is lonely Unaccompanied.
He walks stiffly, and wears his coat
As though he wishes it to shrink,
Indeed it is tough, knotted but comfortable.

I retreat empty handed with grass stains
On my elbows and knees.
A shallow grunting whinny and soluble eyes
Watch me tread.
I turn, smile, giving him confidence,
He concentrates on the silhouetted landscape,
And knows I will return.

Beverley Peel (14)

Beverley is coining phrases, not for show, or to approximate some ideal of poetic diction, but out of need: her desire to articulate something marvellous in the personality of the horse she has befriended and her imaginative explorations into the horse's past life, produce strong, simple phrases. She does not appear to be inhibited by any grand misconceptions about the medium. She is not insensitive to form and rhythm, however, and has a feel for the power of repeated patterns of sentence-making, and for pace. She saw that poetry was simply a means of recording her response to the world, which offered her scope to bring her feelings into consciousness, define them sharply and share them.

Initial misconceptions could be summarised as follows:

– poetry is effeminate
– poetry is for white 'toffs', not for those of low social status or for those from minority groups
– poetry is anything that looks like a poem
– poetry expresses exalted and/or profoundly sympathetic sentiments
– poetry uses specially beautiful words
– poetry is a word game, the manipulation of complicated extended metaphors.

– poetry distils wisdom and truth.

This last 'misconception' represents a substantial problem: poetry's way of communication has been interpreted in terms derived from the different way of communicating used in rational discourse. These two kinds of language use need to be distinguished.

'Poetry Distils Wisdom and Truth'

Unless they read a lot of literature our pupils are surrounded by didactic discourses: the informative and rational essay-writing culture of school academic subjects, and the journalism of newspapers and broadcasting. These works describe, analyse, evaluate, judge, draw conclusions, draw up plans for action, discriminate between alternatives, and act. They use language from a viewpoint that is outside the subject. Poetry uses a very different kind of discourse. Poetry is not concerned with useful conclusions or with action or rather, if it is, it works indirectly by moving the reader/listener with an experience of reality, not by telling them what conclusions should be drawn, what action to take, or what 'the answer' is. It shows, it does not tell. Poetry *can* express a kind of wisdom and truth, but not in discursive terms that can be directly extrapolated from the poem. Young writers need reminding that the way of poetry is the way of concretising not abstracting; of *being* the parts of the subject, not analysing them; of selecting significant detail, not summarising the whole; of inspired glimpses of similarity with other logically unrelated areas of knowledge through imagery.

For someone to write:

OLD AGE

I feel sorry for old people
I can imagine what it must be like
My heart goes out to them, etc.

would be commendable evidence of goodwill, and would perhaps accurately report their feelings, but it does little to put the reader through the experience that gave rise to those feelings and recreate them. It is too much on the outside to be effective poetry. The experiences, thoughts and feelings have been processed, digested, and the conclusions are being reported to us. For someone to write:

Old age is loneliness
Old age is full of memories
Old age is slow and sad
etc.

might again represent commendable goodwill and be the work
of a decent, caring person, but it would be bad poetry. It operates
at a level of generalisation that is fatuous, by taking on a theme
of importance ('Old Age') rather than a particular felt experience.
It tries to make generalisations (appropriate, if at all, to a
discursive medium) seem moving and profound simply by
dressing them in the borrowed robes of poetry's potent conventions. Generalisation of this kind is a statistical blunt instrument
that takes what is thought to be a common or majority experience
and elevates it into a universal *state*. One of the first rules in the
teaching of poetry writing, especially to adolescents who have
developed a taste for the universal and ideal, is to avoid
abstractions and to cut the last four lines of a poem that generalise
the conclusion. Say to the class, 'Let the poem speak for itself.
Do not summarise for it.' Give them the slogan, 'Show, don't
tell.'

The following, humbler, piece about an old person, by an 11
year old, however hesitant and unpolished, *is* unmistakably a
form of poetry and not an artified essay:

POEM FOR A PAINTING
BY PICASSO

Only one woman
In olden times
Wearing an old cloak
Just stood
Looking at something, someone
She looks dull
And not very happy
She looks kind
And I feel sorry for her
I think she is honest
The dull sadness look on her face
I like this woman
On her left ear
One ear ring
Her hair is grey
And pulled back

Her left eye has faded
She cannot see
Sadness in her smile.

Margaret Neilson (11)

Reading this you gain a definite impression that Margaret has had an engrossing, imaginative experience, and that she is managing to record it. It has no pretentions to knowledge about old age. It is formally plain and adequate, but in a fairly rudimentary state. Some opportunities for tighter patterning and for irony, particularly with the 'looking at something, someone' and the 'she cannot see' relationship, have been missed, which a more formally aware writer would work on in a second draft, but it does recreate an experience for us and bring a character to life before our eyes.

'Poetry is Obscure'

We are now going to consider the misconceptions which do not so much worry young children as afflict students of literature from the teenage years up and still have a tenacious hold on many teachers. The belief that poetry is impenetrably obscure is based on a number of factors and we can understand it better if we break it down into its constituent parts.

Poetry contains ridiculously erudite and obscure references

Teachers and examiners, partly because of the demands of the 'practical criticism' method, often choose predominantly 'difficult' Modernist texts for study (along with a few 'difficult' earlier writers, notably John Donne, revived by T. S. Eliot's critical liking for them). An Eliot, Ezra Pound, David Jones, Wallace Stevens or James Joyce text *is* a fiendishly obscure and referential puzzle. An Eliot poem, for example, may contain references to Dante (in Italian), to Aeschylus (in Greek), to Classical, Norse, Arthurian, Amerindian mythologies, to Cellini, Fra Angelico, Baedecker guides, and all the knowledge of a man of leisure who has spent a life as an aesthete, a scholar and a traveller. The vocabulary is often way beyond that of even the best read 17 year old A level student and seems perversely paraded. The fact that the bulk of the world's poetry over the centuries has been accessible and highly entertaining on a first

reading is not something you would ever guess from taking
literature courses in some British secondary schools. It is only
since the French *symbolistes*, and then Pound and Eliot following
them, that obscurity has been cultivated as style, and pride taken
in making extreme demands upon the reader.

Eliot himself gives a charmingly coquettish account of the
inscrutability of the artist in his *Old Possum* poem 'The Naming
of Cats'. After telling us about each cat's *family* name and
particular name he tells us about its third name:

> But above and beyond there's still one name left over,
>   And that is the name that you never will guess;
> The name that no human research can discover –
>   But THE CAT HIMSELF KNOWS, and will never confess.
> When you notice a cat in profound meditation,
>   The reason, I tell you, is always the same:
> His mind is engaged in a rapt contemplation
>   Of the thought, of the thought, of the thought of his name:
>   His ineffable effable
>   Effanineffable
> Deep and inscrutable singular Name.

These fat cats are invariably Modernist poets and critics. They
have professionalised literature, which used to belong to everybody. The audience for Homer and the Greek tragedians, for
folk songs, for Corpus Christi plays, for Shakespeare's early
plays, and for hymns was the whole community.

The 'conspiracy' theory of literature

Reading a poem has been turned into a frightening, problematic
activity by our education at O and A level. Many perfectly
capable, intelligent people, good teachers and confident novel
readers, even teachers of literature, have never recovered from
the bruising they took in their early experience of 'learning
poetry'. Judging by the attitudes of student teachers today and
the findings of the HMI report, *A Survey of the Teaching of A
Level English Literature in 20 Mixed Sixth Forms in Comprehensive
Schools* (DES, 1987a), the same teaching methods that led to the
conspiracy theory are still practised in some places.

The teacher, following the educational theory that articulating
each reader's response is the purpose of the process, refuses to
give guidance but tries to elicit 'response' by questioning, and

ends the 'practical criticism' session in one of two ways. If a progressive, the teacher tries to validate each student's response and offer reassurance, saying that the several interpretations are all equally good, that meaning is relative and that images work on many levels. If an educational conservative, the teacher tells the students what the 'right' interpretation was that was being withheld from them while they struggled with partial and inadequate ones.

Either of these approaches may leave the confused student with a sense of having been cheated, and of futility. Why should I sweat to understand it if (a) the meaning is relative and does not matter, or (b) there is always a more correct and more complete answer than mine which I will be given if I just hang on? The recent HMI report on A level English teaching commented that questions from the teacher were sometimes 'narrow or obscure, with a preconceived notion of the "correct" answer, at which students aimed optimistic but erratic guesses'.

Modernist new criticism taught through 'practical criticism' of unseen texts (i.e. discussion classes focused on the interpretation of unattributed poems without any background information about the author or time of composition), which in some ways was like its contemporary discipline, psychoanalysis. Like psychoanalysis, new criticism delighted in the most difficult texts and was bored by the unproblematic. Like psychoanalysis, practical criticism became a sort of super-game which had a private language and attracted a certain kind of intellectual, an addict of speculative interpretation. When living under the shadow of the examination system, such an activity is easily perverted into the parroting of clever imitation criticism for good grades. Those who do not take naturally to such an unnatural activity can end up feeling foolish outsiders in the literary world. New criticism was the theoretical basis for all literature teaching in the British education system for many decades, until very recently.

Poetry deliberately withholds its meaning

Modernist texts are often obscure, but most poems from other periods are not hidden behind surface obscurities, though they may present reading difficulties if the language and cultural references are old and unfamiliar. It is the case, however, that poetry does not use language in the straightforward way we are

used to, and so there is a second order of 'difficulty' in reading
a poem.

Poetry often speaks through images in a non-rational or indirect
way. In a rationalist education system the process of trying to
translate poetic language into rational terms necessarily creates
'difficulty'. Keats wrote to his brothers, George and Tom, that
in the course of a conversation with a friend 'several things
dovetailed in my mind, and at once it struck me, what quality
went to form a Man of Achievement especially in Literature and
which Shakespeare possessed so enormously – I mean *Negative
Capability*, that is when man is capable of being in uncertainties,
Mysteries, doubts, without any irritable reaching after fact and
reason. . .' This *'negative capability'* is a quality possessed by
readers, too, who can accept and savour the strangeness of what
they read without 'irritable reaching' after completed meanings.
It is the non-discursive spirit of the arts.

Reading with *negative capability* is not an easy trick to learn.
It requires the suspension of one's deeply ingrained discursive
method of thought, in which one reads for information, summa-
tions, authoritative judgements, certainties and solutions – in
short, for *knowledge*. Poetry does not characteristically offer
knowledge in a form which can be removed from its context in
the poem. The poem offers an experience. Readers have to be
willing to give themselves to the experience, immerse themselves
in it and savour the reality revealed. Proper criticism comes as
an attempt to report on the reading experience afterwards and
reflect on the special quality of the experience. Examination-
drill criticism has regrettably given people the impression that
criticism means reading-for-judgement, or reading-to-extract-
the-meaning, a procedure which bypasses the immersion-in-the-
experience reading and applies discursive methods inappro-
priately to poetry. To read with negative capability means
suspending judgement, holding contradictory ideas in mind
without needing to plump for one or the other, allowing the
poem to create a whole picture before separating out the parts,
waiting for the aftertaste and the ironies to rise, accepting the
unresolved ambiguities and treating the poem as a complete
independent being, not something to argue with or *use*.

Discursive language proceeds by argument, on the assumption
that words refer to things out there in the world and that through
the language we can grasp the reality. The language of poetry is
'foregrounded', i.e. draws attention to itself more than functional

language used for conveying information does, so each statement intended to represent the reality more directly becomes another linguistic mask for what can never quite be said in language. The 'meaning' is inseparable from the words chosen. Discursive language is a problem-solving medium, moving through analysis towards 'solutions'. In a more familiar scientific form it is the language of 'diagnosis' and 'cure'.

In everyday discursive language a situation might be defined thus: '*I feel exhausted, have pains in my chest, I fidget and I cannot concentrate; I lose my temper for no reason; I look out of the window and burst into tears; I expect it is the loss, but who is to blame? If I try and keep working hard I could keep my pain at bay perhaps. . .*' etc. In poetic language the same situation might be rendered thus:

> Break, break, break,
>   At the foot of thy crags, O Sea!
> But the tender grace of a day that is dead
>   Will never come back to me.

> (from 'Break, Break, Break',
> Alfred Lord Tennyson)

Poetic language is used to evoke a state, not to cure it out of existence. The word 'break' is opaque. It is a metaphor appealing to certain emotional associations of the sea and of violent futile movement. It draws to itself all the clutter of 'symptoms' above and all our individual memories of sadness, and becomes a sign for them that is much more satisfying than a phrase like 'separation syndrome' because it is not trying to sort anything out, it just *is*. The words are there not so much for what they precisely refer to in a discursive sense (or 'denote') – the waves seen on the shore one day when Tennyson was out walking – but for their wider associations and emotional flavour (what they 'connote') – a broken heart, a bitter sense of destruction. The words also 'enact' their subject in a way that discursive language does not. 'Break, break, break' *is* a hard and broken thing to say. The movement of the lips from the '*k*' word-ending to the '*br*' forces a 'break' in speaking; it is a monotonous, slow-paced line and its sound is 'an echo to the sense'. The line is not at all difficult to understand, but it is difficult, if not impossible, to render all its 'meaning' in a discursive prose equivalent. If you approach it with a discursive examination question mentality and ask what it 'means', then unless you are already critically sophisticated and happy playing with conundrums, you will get bogged down, lose your negative capability and frustrate yourself.

By ancient tradition, songs or poems are complete in themselves – you do not argue with them – and the fact that a Tennyson lyric (or a blues song, or whatever) is a complete thing, outside the realm of discursive thought, with a reassuringly rounded structure, can give a 'wholeness' to the experience of receiving it and a feeling that it encapsulates profound 'truth'. But you cannot reach through the word 'break' and grasp that 'truth', paraphrasing it into rational language, laying bare the reality; it is a function of the whole form of the lyric and of its status in the privileged discourse of art. A poem or song is not difficult to enjoy, to be moved by, or to be impressed by, but it becomes 'difficult' in the process of criticism unless you are very clear in your mind about the distinction between criticism and its discursive mode, and poetry and its connotative, enacting mode. The misconception that *poetry withholds its meaning* is the other side of the same coin as *poetry distils wisdom and truth*. Both arise from critical approaches that concentrate on trying to abstract the 'meaning' of a poem in a way that creates false expectations and forgets Keats' strictures on the acceptance of 'uncertainties, Mysteries, doubts'.

Poetry can also be found 'difficult', or rather 'undiscursive', in that it circles around the theme and eschews direct statement. Compare a less than successful Wordsworth lyric with a magnificent old ballad. This is the second and last stanza of a famous 'Lucy' poem:

> She lived unknown, and few could know
>   When Lucy ceased to be;
> But she is in her grave, and, oh,
>   The difference to me!

The word 'difference' has to work very hard to carry the great load of grief Wordsworth is giving it because it is too direct. As it does so it trips over its own toes, induced by the rhythm to stretch itself portentously to three full syllables. But, most dismaying, it breaks the unwritten conventions of literary decorum and plonks a load of raw feeling in the reader's lap. What am I supposed to do with this? You feel.

Compare this with the power and poignancy of a poem of death in which the notion of grief is so resolutely absent that the hole in the centre where humane feeling ought to be swells to engulf the reader.

THE TWA CORBIES

As I was walking all alane
I heard twa corbies* making a mane;
The tane unto the t'other say,
'Where sall we gang dine today?'

' – In behint yon auld fail dyke,
I wot there lies a new-slain Knight;
And naebody kens that he lies there,
But his hawk, his hound, and lady fair.

'His hound is to the hunting gane,
His hawk to fetch the wild-fowl hame,
His lady's ta'en another mate,
So we may mak' our dinner sweet.

'Ye'll sit on his white hause-bane,
And I'll pick out his bonny blue een:
Wi' ae lock o' his gowden hair
We'll theek our nest when it grows bare.

'Mony a one for him makes mane,
But none sall ken where he is gane;
O'er his white banes, when they are bare,
The wind sall blaw for evermair.'

Anon.

'The Twa Corbies' is not difficult to read or receive once you have worked out the Scots dialect variants of 'two', 'alone', 'moan', 'home', 'eyes' and begun to thrill to its special sound quality, culminating in the unforgettable open windy vowels of the last line. Not difficult to receive, no, although it certainly is perverse in that it concentrates on the opposite of what it means. This is not the same as obscurity because the reader readily apprehends the significance of the repetitions of callousness and knows what it is that the poem circles around, like a vulture not yet settled on its subject. The lip-smacking carrion crows, for all their appalling complacency about death, present in a grisly form all those qualities so lacking in the Knight – sharing, helping, humour, and joy – parodying their absence.

The only bad line is the one which comes too close to the deliberately avoided statement: 'Mony a one for him makes

---

Corbies – carrion crows; *fail dyke* – turf wall; *hause-bane* – breast bone

mane'. It is the only line which is not imaginatively visualised
in the concrete but leads you away into vagueness. If his hawk,
hound and lady are not grieving, then who are the 'mony a one'?
The distinctive strength of the poem is the bleak absence of ties
of affection.

Wei T'ai, an eleventh century Chinese poet, wrote:

> Poetry presents the thing in order to convey the feeling. It should
> be precise about the thing and reticent about the feeling, for as
> soon as the mind responds and connects with the thing the feeling
> shows in the words; this is how poetry enters deeply into us. If
> the poet presents directly feelings which overwhelm him, and keeps
> nothing back to linger as an aftertaste, he stirs us superficially.

The 'thing' in this case is the image of the crows. They are
vividly and precisely rendered and the Knight's tragedy speaks
through them, all the louder for being mute.

There are many kinds of poetry, some of which are actually
didactic in purpose like Pope's *Essays* or Thompson's *Seasons*,
and some of which are openly confessional like Coleridge's
Dejection: A Letter. But poetic expression is most often indirect
and reveals itself by taking a detour through repetitive transformations of the (absent) theme. As the semiotician, Michael
Riffaterre, has put it:

> The text functions something like a neurosis: as the matrix is
> repressed, the displacement produces variants all through the text,
> just as suppressed symptoms break out somewhere else in the
> body. (Riffaterre, 1978)

The text, though circuitous and coy, is not inscrutable. It is full
of patterned repetitions, variants, and transformations – what in
linguistics is called a 'redundancy' in the message. It is built to
last, 'and rests upon so many intricate relationships that it is
relatively impervious to change and deterioration of the linguistic
code' (Riffaterre, 1978). Literature is not a transparent window
on meanings, but only when it is playing games is it effanineffable.

The conclusion I wish to draw from this discussion is that
although reading poetry is different from reading discursive prose
and requires that you turn the phrases over in your mind, as you
would turn in your hand polished stones, and savour them
without 'irritable reaching after fact and reason', it is in fact an
accessible, and infinitely pleasurable activity if you can overcome

your sense of the conspiracy. Ian Coffey, an Irish poet, has said,
'. . . one has to give a poem an attention similar to that one gives
to a conversation with a new friend' (in Egan and Hartnett,
1978).

The Tangled Aims of Studying Literature

The misconception that poetry is impenetrably obscure is partly
due to the fact that Modernist poetry often *is* obscure; partly
due to confusion between the discursive discourse of criticism
and poetic discourse; and partly due to confusion in the aims of
literature teaching, which is what we turn to now.

The curriculum in this country has been determined from the
top down, by the entry requirements of degree courses, and O
and A levels have been designed in the past to prepare students
for further specialist study, not primarily as inducements to *enjoy*
literature, develop personal communication skills and explore its
content, as opposed to its form.

Academic critical writing tends to focus on the rhetoric of
literary artifice and rarely engages with themes directly in the
way that non-specialist readers like to do. (How often in all the
millions of words written about *Othello* or *Macbeth* have you
come across comments like, 'When I was jealous of my wife. . .',
or, 'When I was ambitious to oust the ageing professor in our
department. . .'?) Academic research explores a text's relationships with other areas of knowledge: with the writer's culture
and personal history; with the history of the language; with the
history of literary forms; with the history of society (and often
with theoretical accounts, such as Marxism and feminism); with
literary theory or linguistic theory; with philosophy and with
other arts.

The teacher of literature may be trying to cover one or more
of these areas of knowledge with the class, and in addition will
be trying to incorporate educational aims into the lessons. This
can lead to a muddle: is one teaching pupils to appreciate art, or
to be rationally analytical? Is the aim the development of
'sensibility' ('careful articulation of thought and feeling', as HMI
put it), an understanding of cultural history, a knowledge of
literary genres and techniques, a refined taste and judgement, a
trained skill in discussion? Is one teaching pupils how to write
an essay or giving a moral lesson on, for example, the inhumanity
of war or of the oppression of women?

Teachers have sometimes attempted all these things without sorting out priorities and it is not surprising that pupils have become confused. As social theorists analysing the 'hidden curriculum' have shown, we may not even have been doing what we thought we were doing. Literary criticism is the subject which above all others is open to the charge that it has been part of a social mechanism to recruit for an élite, distinguished from uncultured persons by its mastery of the superior discourse of 'taste' and its knowledge of the Establishment's canon of masterpieces.

It will help us to see a way through the confusion if, firstly, we distinguish what is appropriate for specialists from what is appropriate in a general education for those aged 8 to 16. Secondly, we should put *writing literature* at the centre of our plans alongside *reading literature*. Thirdly, we should start from the question, 'What are the pupil's needs?' rather than the question, 'What are the important truths about literature?' These three themes constitute the agenda for the next chapter.

2 Clearing Away Misconceptions

In this chapter I shall first briefly review the literature teaching strategies which are appropriate in a general education, then consider the place of *writing* in the curriculum – in relation to literature and to the development of thinking – and finally propose a rationale for the drafting of poetry.

The Teaching of Literature

There are ways in which poetry can be taught so that it does not create anxiety and feelings of inadequacy. Some schools set a fine example and bring literature alive: they invite writers into the classroom, run book festivals, join with other local schools for poetry readings, use playful and creative approaches to exploring literature and recognise that criticism is an open enquiry, not a body of received opinions. This book is not about the teaching of criticism in the secondary school so I shall do no more here than indicate some of the strategies good literature teachers use with young people in their general education to avoid creating the impression that they are conspiring to humiliate, and to sort out the confusions resulting from tangled teaching aims.

The teacher can practise creative exercises that build confidence by involving students in the construction and realisation of the text – transformations, reconstructions, extensions and dramatisations – and by using teacherless discussion groups. Peter Benton's *Pupil, Teacher, Poem* quotes very impressive evidence from teacherless discussion groups and demonstrates how effective this technique for exploring literature can be.

Simply reading a lot and *enjoying* literature should be high on the list of priorities, leaving extensive formal analysis to those who later choose to specialise. If you spend less time on analysis you can get three times as much reading done!

The popular non-specialist appeal of literature has always been made up of several elements: entertainment; the fact that literature gives rise to discussion of feelings, of characters, of ideas, and of ethical issues; the sensual pleasure of naming things, of using the tactile qualities of words, and of patterned rhythms; the sheer brilliance of witty observations, memorable phrases, strikingly expressed ideas and thrilling images. In the education of non-specialist 8 to 16 year olds, the emphasis should be on these aspects of literature rather than on pale imitations of specialist structural and rhetorical analysis.

To avoid giving the impression that poetry is effete, middle-class and overwhelmingly a white British cultural product, the selection of texts should be varied and multicultural. A class can look at examples of verse which reflect differing views of what a poem is, and discuss them. Use poems by children as well as published poems. For the sake of winning over reluctant readers, there might have to be some positive discrimination in your selection in the early days towards establishing poetry's credentials as non-precious. Poetry needs saving from the literary museum. It needs some of its passion restored to it, and its irreverent and satirical spirit, its lustiness, comedy, morbid sensationalism, and its power to disturb your sleep. Luckily, Baldwin's anthology of 'tough' verse, *Billy the Kid*, the robust popular writing of Michael Rosen, Kit Wright and Shel Silverstein, Causley's anthologies of *Salt Sea Verse* and *Magic Verse*, Summerfields's superb *Voices* anthologies, collections of oral verse, collections of Caribbean verse such as *Bluefoot Traveller* and *Caribbean Poetry Now*, Mansfield and Armstrong's *A Sudden Line*, Heaney and Hughes' *The Rattle Bag*, the Bentons' *Poetry Workshop* books, more recently the Brownjohns' *Meet and Write* and Orme and Sale's *The Poetry Show*, and many other fine anthologies, have already blazed a trail, so the problem of preciousness is not now as acute for the younger generation as it was for teachers educated before these developments.

Introducing pupils to lively, funny and dramatic poems will set a good example and help to combat misconceptions concerning the subject matter, diction and style of poetry. With the older pupils you can address the issue directly: poetry is not one style and it embraces such contrasting creatures as Tennyson, D. H. Lawrence, and William Carlos Williams:

SONG – THE OWL

When cats run home and light is come,
   And dew is cold upon the ground,
And the far-off stream is dumb,
   And the whirring sail goes round,
   And the whirring sail goes round:
      Alone and warming his five wits,
      The white owl in the belfry sits.

When merry milkmaids click the latch,
   And rarely smells the new-mown hay,
And the cock hath sung beneath the thatch
   Twice or thrice his roundelay,
   Twice or thrice his roundelay;
      Alone and warming his five wits,
      The white owl in the belfry sits.

                  Alfred Lord Tennyson

PEACH

Would you like to throw a stone at me?
Here, take all that's left of my peach.

Blood-red, deep;
Heaven knows how it came to pass.
Somebody's pound of flesh rendered up.

Wrinkled with secrets
And hard with the intention to keep them.

Why, from silvery peach-bloom,
From that shallow-silvery wine-glass on a short stem
This rolling, dropping, heavy globule?
I am thinking, of course, of the peach before I ate it.

Why so velvety, why so voluptuous heavy?
Why hanging with such inordinate weight
Why so indented?

Why the groove?
Why the lovely, bivalve roundnesses?
Why the ripple down the sphere?
Why the suggestion of incision?

Why was not my peach round and finished like a
billiard ball?
It would have been if man had made it.
Though I've eaten it now.

But it wasn't round and finished like a billiard ball.
And because I say so, you would like to throw
something at me.

Here, you can have my peach stone.

                                            D. H. Lawrence

THE LOCUST TREE IN FLOWER

Among
of
green

stiff
old
bright

broken
branch
come

white
sweet
May

again

                            William Carlos Williams

Each of the above poems is on a stereotypically 'poetic' subject,
the beauty of some aspect of nature. It is not the subject which
makes the Lawrence poem sound so aggressively offhand, daring,
and informal in tone after the elegant dance of Tennyson. In
fact, the contrast between the subject and the manner makes the
Lawrence poem a very odd thing indeed: the speech challenges
you to a fight, harangues you, pops in patronising conversational
afterthoughts ('I am thinking, of course, of the peach before I
ate it'), brandishing its swaggering modernity at you as if to defy
you to call poetry cissy. At the same time he relishes the down
on a peach with that supersensitivity that is part of the popular
comic stereotype of a poet that Pope satirised in his 'Essay on
Man':

> To smart and agonise at every pore?
> Or quick effluvia darting through the brain,
> Die of a rose in aromatic pain?

It manages to suggest that this peach-drooling is an energetic and sexy occupation, but the trick is in the language, the argumentative bar-room talk rhythms, and the tension remains; the poem is the converse of a peach: an egg with a hard brittle surface and a soft inside. But this apparently casual and quarrelsome voice, scattered in short lines, blunt demands and occasional flights of heady eloquence is a voice that can be a fine model of uninhibited language for pupils to imitate. It is close to speech, though strongly rhetorical.

The William Carlos Williams poem is modernity of a different kind, without the rhetorical flourish, apparently stripped to the structural basics. It will not immediately appeal to most pupils; it is too unhelpful in its syntax. But if they can get over the strangeness of it and come to recognise its special awkward charm, they can see that anything is possible and be emboldened to take liberties with language themselves.

The aim of the discussion of these poems is not to condemn the honeyed melody of Tennyson and exalt modern colloquial speech but rather to show that both are legitimate languages and that one can use what language one chooses.

Teaching Through Writing

Learning about the construction of an effective text is much better done with non-specialists through *writing* than through critical analysis. It has the further advantage that writing is a skill whose usefulness they can appreciate, whereas literary criticism is not. The understanding of craft and construction that develops through writing leads to a more realistic appreciation of the achievements of literary authors. The critical confusions are not such a problem when one is writing. One is in the middle of the activity, using the artistic medium and all its rhetorical skills and its *genre* conventions. Pupils may not be able to write clearly about knotty issues in aesthetic philosophy, but if they can write poems then they 'know' a lot about poetry and have a vital relationship with literature. Take the relationship between form and meaning. Most approaches to this through critical discussion raise more questions than they answer (quite naturally) and leave the pupil floundering. Yet critically unsophisticated pupils can *use* complex formal means to express themselves with intuitive skill:

TWO

Shall we
yes
climb into my web

Tony Nelson   (16)

The broken syntax of speech *is* a large part of the meaning of this poem, which, like Ted Hughes' '*The Thought-Fox*', represents an idea suddenly coming sharply into focus. Tony could no more articulate this relationship as an abstract conception than Maradona could explain the physiology of muscle fibre. They do not need to if they can perform effectively. But Tony's level of critical awareness could be developed through discussion of his own work *linked to critical reading* more effectively than through work on literary texts alone.

I do not wish to argue for ignorance and against criticism, but for a more central role for literary writing, and for the integration of the reading and the writing of literature. Tony could be encouraged to examine his own writing in a quite different spirit from that in which he could be asked to explain the operation of syntax and metaphor in a sonnet by Wordsworth. There would be a motivating curiosity at work in his trying to account for why he made certain choices in writing his poem. He would be dealing with a phenomenon that was mysterious in a genuinely 'open' sense. He would know from the start that no one could be a greater authority on his work than himself, and could confidently judge between alternative accounts of what he had done on the basis of whether they 'felt' right or not. It is true that criticising Wordsworth is also an 'open' activity, but to most pupils it will not *seem* so, and they will be less curious and much less confident about their judgements. They will have the impression that 'understanding Wordsworth' is an already established body of knowledge which they are supposed to try and clumsily recreate. They will see the sense in understanding Wordsworth's use of language better if they come to it after trying to describe their own, and in the same spirit.

Football is still taught through playing it; art is taught through doing it, and dance through dancing; but literature is taught through criticism, and language is often taught through 'knowledge about language' and the practice of isolated skills. A separation of theory and practice has arisen in English: in many places the reading of literature is divorced from the writing of stories and poems. As a consequence the literature is perceived as more 'difficult' and obscure than it really is, the difficulty being a condition of critical debate rather than a necessary feature of literary production.

Reading poetry is a more comprehensible activity if it is part of the same study as writing poetry. A proliferation of academic 'isms' has left the theoretical basis for literature teaching a subject of raging controversy, and theory leads in many different directions (some of which never return to literature) as we saw in the last chapter. Dogen wrote in the thirteenth century:

> If there were a bird who first wanted to examine the size of the sky, or a fish who first wanted to examine the extent of the water – and then to try to fly or swim, they will never find their own ways in the sky or water.

He was right: the best way round the conceptual problems is to plunge right in! Write!

Amuse yourself with Disgusting Poems, Anti-Poetry Poems, Punk Poems and Dialect Poems in order to subvert the misconceptions about subject matter, noble sentiments and style – but beware of setting up a new misconception, that *modern* poetry should be about the brutality of a Nooligan, as Roger McGough calls his character.

PUNK LOVE

I went for a walk with Barry the other day,
Down the alley that leads to the station,
He gave me a fag and right then I knew it was love
So we sprayed our names in spray paint, all up the walls
   How romantic. . .

When I'm a decrepit old fart,
I'll walk down here and remember,
Remember the happy times we spent
Smashing up bottles and frightening old bags,
   How romantic. . .

Allison Blay (13)

US DREADS

In a dis ya skool
us dreads rool.
Soul head dem saaf
mek us dreads laugh
dem no no how fe dress
but us dreads strickly de bess.
Gal dem cool an
control dem part ah de skool.
Mek us dreads feel sweet
each day ah de week.
Teachers all weird
mek saaf buoy scared
but us dread move together
an control de skool.
De music we play
nice up de day.
Rythdym just nice it
Teacher dem no like it.
When exam come
some dreads run
dem carn do dem tings.
In de enn teachar dem win.
Us dreads carn get na wok
we strickly brok
lose out in de enn
but us dreads still frienn.

Dave Martin (16)

One of the most effective methods of clearing away misconceptions without getting caught up in a rarefied discussion of what poetry is and what it is not (which would be more likely to confuse than to clarify pupils' thinking) is to launch straight into a Group Poem (see Chapter 5). It needs no introduction and immediately teaches that pupils *can* do an honest, accurate piece of observational writing and that obscure rules of rhyme and rhythm do not enter the case. They will be surprised and, in some cases, shocked, to discover that they have written a 'poem', that it was an unmysterious process and relatively painless (you can do it all without mentioning the word poem). Some will still not think the result is a 'proper' poem, but that can lead you nicely into a discussion of their received ideas that can be very helpful in the process of clarification.

As pupils are always looking for clues as to what the teacher's demands really mean, and what will satisfy him or her, you might as well give plenty of clues when you respond to writing and say what you value. Honesty and clarity are the values at the top of my scale of priorities for young writers. These are not absolute criteria for judging poetry or the performance of pupils, but they are commonly preferred in our generation. Other ages have had good reason to value piety or intricate decorative skill in verse-making, but we tend to value what everyone can do well: simple, honest expression.

Drafting in the Curriculum

Poetry is not a fringe activity; nor is it just one of the many arts subjects. It is the art of language, and the art of language is more important than the other arts in education because language is the medium for thinking and communicating in all areas of life. Through the practice of the art of language one teaches thinking.

Let us take a long perspective on the aims of language development programmes. Employers' associations – commercial, industrial, technical and public employers – emphasise again and again that they are less interested in particular areas of knowledge or technical accomplishment than in what are now called in the jargon 'transferable personal skills'. They want people who can *think*, who can adapt to new situations, solve problems, work with others and communicate well. The stereotype of unenlightened employers who want obedient factory fodder is happily now out of date and the skills and understandings we value as educationalists are in demand. The CBI calls for education to attach 'greater weight to personal qualities such as motivation, ability for original thought and ability to solve problems'. A joint statement by the *University Grants Committee and the National Advisory Body for Local Authority Higher Education* summarises these new skills:

> The abilities most valued in industrial, commercial and professional life as well as in public and social administration are the transferable intellectual and personal skills. These include the ability to analyse complex issues, to identify the core of the problem and the means of solving it, to synthesise and integrate disparate elements, to clarify values, to make effective use of numerical and other information, to work cooperatively and

constructively with others, and, above all perhaps, to communicate clearly both orally and in writing.

What does poetry writing teach? Poetry is language at its most concentrated, where every word counts. It teaches clarity and economy of expression; close observation, accuracy and truth to experience; making an impact with words 'realising' the subject matter in a fully imagined and concrete form; control over language – the solving of problems such as identifying the core of the subject, focusing and ordering within an appropriate structure (see Chapter 3 for illustrations of this process); sensitivity in the choice of words; awareness of the audience response. As transferable intellectual and communication skills of universal application, these are not bad for a start. Poetry writing is a more effective way of approaching communication skills than language drills and comprehension exercises because the highest level of 'comprehension' is to find just the right word with all the connotative qualities that suit the purpose and a writer is working at the cutting edge of language to do just that. These skills are developed not as technical accomplishments for their own sakes, in isolation, in a mechanical way, but as a byproduct of respecting the integrity of the art of poetry. One does not set out to teach a thinking skill; one sets out to involve pupils in crafting a poem or song. But this necessarily involves them in the rigorous discipline of drafting.

The drafting process is absolutely central to education – it is how we make progress in thinking. But how does *thinking* relate to *feeling* and the development of 'the whole person'? To emphasise *thinking* is not to reduce all activities to the cognitive and ignore other areas of experience, but to say that education is primarily concerned with making things conscious and articulating them. The things articulated may well be feelings, or intutitions, or portions of raw experience. The relationship between thinking and life is best expressed by that profoundest of thinkers, William Blake: 'Reason is the bound or outward circumference of Energy.' By 'Energy' I take him to mean all the activity of life, the creativity, the feelings and motivating force. Reason is at the defining edge. It is not the creative force, not the power unit in life, but it is where Energy is defined in language and can be understood. Education takes place at this circumference, and the best way to educate is to collaborate in drafting language to express the 'Energy'. To do this well requires great sensitivity to the emotional, spiritual, or intuitive aspects of life one tries to understand and describe – the greater the sensitivity the more subtle the consciousness that develops and the better the thinking. The task which develops subtlety and sensitivity of thought is working on making the outline of Energy as sharply perceived as possible.

There are several elements to sharp perception. One is the complex of activities associated with *articulation*: there is observation, which in science and the visual arts takes a high proportion of the time and has its special techniques; and there is description, which will involve analysis and evaluation if the medium is discursive prose, and imaginative 'realisation' if the medium is poetry or fiction.

The other element is *awareness* which also has more than one aspect. The first concerns the context. You cannot perceive anything really sharply in school if you do not know why you are there, what the point is of what you are asked to do, or how the subject matter relates to your life. This form of awareness is the subject of Chapter 10.

Another aspect is *being conscious of yourself using your mind*. For example, pupils can learn a successful strategy, but not realise what it is that they have learned and not be able to call upon it again in another context – for that they have to have an abstract conception of their control over thinking structures. We need to keep reminding them explicitly what strategies they are using, as they add to their repertoire of language and thinking skills. This form of awareness is the subject of Margaret Donaldson's classic of educational psychology, *Children's Minds*. She states her theme like this:

> If the intellectual powers are to develop, the child must gain a measure of control over his own thinking and he cannot control it while he remains unaware of it. The attaining of this control means prising thought out of its primitive unconscious embeddedness in the immediacies of living in the world and interacting with other human beings.

I discuss the issue of 'disembedding' thinking in the course of commenting on a pupil's writing drafts in Chapter 3.

Another form of awareness is *the bringing into focus, the drawing into consciousness, of half-perceived feelings*. This, too, is shown in Chapter 3.

It should be apparent from this account of the elements that make up *thinking* that I am not using the term to refer to rationalist, analytical thought alone, and that the aim of teaching *thinking* in this sense is not incompatible with the aim of developing 'the whole person'. The choice of the word *thinking* is intended, however, to emphasise that the mischievous notion that the teacher's rôle is to be a social worker, to compensate for lack of parenting, or to be a glorified childminder, leads us away from our aims. Teachers fulfil many rôles, but their main function is to teach – to develop the consciousness of the pupil.

Why Poetry?

What characteristics does poetry have that make it ideally suited to the teaching of thinking? Why is poetry appropriate for drafting? Because poems are short. Because poems are personal – a perception, an idea, a feeling, an experience. And because poems are, by cultural convention, a form of public communication that enables one to turn a personal perception into something for admiration. These features make poetry the most accessible written genre for young pupils and the most amenable for learning language and thinking skills through drafting.

The brevity means that writing a poem does not have to be a test of endurance, with all the organisational complexity of narrative or discursive writing. It can bring quick, encouraging results at all levels of ability and can be redrafted without excessive physical labour. The time may come very soon when pupils have access to word processors for their narrative and discursive writing – let us hope so – but until it does, redrafting long texts is formidably time-consuming and laborious. I believe this is the main reason why the drafting process has not become common practice in schools. Many poems arrive nearly complete. I would not want to give the impression that perfectly good pieces of writing have to be stripped down and reconstructed out of deference to the 'drafting' ideology. Poems, however, are small language constructs that are *crafted*, and the principle of crafting can be kept in the foreground when working with poems without it ever becoming a tedious routine or seeming an expense of great effort on an unworthy object.

The personal nature of poetic writing means that it is, like the diary, the anecdote, and autobiographical narrative, very well suited to pupils before they are ready for analytical intellectual tasks. It continues into the secondary school years as a bridge between experience and objective forms of academic writing.

Poetry is an art and by convention is shared with an audience. Pupils can consequently experience success through poetry; they can share their perceptions with others, receive praise and confirmation of their views. The conventions of the art have two further important characteristics: they provide enabling formal structures to give support to the writer (these are discussed at length in the practical sections in Part Two); and they protect the writer's right to 'fictionalise' personal material, to not be identified with the subject of the poem. The poem is an extremely useful convention for the classroom in that highly personal and intimate subject matter, once it is in verse form, is privileged. You can accept from a pupil a poem of murderous hatred or agonising despair and celebrate its power and eloquence.

The lyric genre is in a curious relationship with its audience anyway. Lyrics do not address the reader directly: they pretend that they do not have a reader. They have the appearance of being private, addressed to the Muse, to a flower, to God, or they are words thrown into the night sky by lovers who dare not utter their thoughts aloud. We, as readers, feel we have stumbled upon something we should not really be reading.

Whether or not it is possible to 'prove' the theory of the cathartic or therapeutic function of the arts, I certainly have an intuitive faith that the expression of painful feelings and the sharing of them with others, under the protection of 'fictionalisation' and the 'you are not really reading this' convention, is satisfying and soothing.

Poetry in schools is not *just* an art, in the sense of a luxury, a bit of the curriculum kept on one side for the 'affective' or 'leisure' aspects of life. Nor are the other arts. Poetry writing is a valuable classroom activity at three levels.

It is *always* a craft, a thinking process that gives experience of controlling language and developing articulacy for everyone, even the most literal minded or the least able.

It is *often* a social process of shared entertainment and shared experience.

And it is *sometimes* an art-making process, when the unpredictable magic happens and new life is brought into being, a surprising 'globed fruit', as Archibald MacLeish has called it, is suddenly before you.

But I would argue that the achievements of average and less

able children in particular, who make significant progress in controlling the medium and organising their thinking, such as some of those quoted in Chapter 3, are important not because they result in the ineffable miracle called art, but because they so clearly result in learning.

It is a wonderful bonus when a really creative work of art appears, like 'Methuselah' quoted in Chapter 1, but the classroom teacher needs to know why the activity is valuable for all, at what is often a fairly pedestrian level of achievement. It is not much help to quote child masterpieces and say, 'Go and do thou likewise' (which is what HMI are in danger of doing in their 1987 publication *Teaching Poetry in the Secondary School*, DES, 1987b). Drafting ought to be central to all education, and poetry is the most appropriate written medium for practising it with children in the middle years. It does not depend upon the production of wonderful works of art for its justification any more than educational science depends upon new discoveries – the works of art are the icing on the cake!

In poetry teaching we are working through an art form, achieving affection for and insights into the art form, and getting to the point where some pupils are writing poems which show remarkable sensitivity and internal coherence. But in spite of this I would assert that our primary purpose is to further the overall aim of education, which is the *development of thinking*, the never-ending task of drawing the defining outline of 'Energy'. To summarise the argument: criticism, understanding literary methods, comprehension, clear language use, clear thinking and 'language awareness' are all more effectively taught through drafting writing than through separate skills exercises. The key to improving quality through drafting is the teacher in the role of critical reader and this role is the subject of the next chapter.

3 Readers Make Writers: How to Tutor a Pupil's Draft

Poetry lives wherever words, however humble and shy, are expected to have meaning and considered to be worth looking at again. As soon as this condition is seen to be fulfilled in a classroom, poetry will spring up, and it will continue to flourish because the communication established is so gratifying it is its own reward. Poetry is there in abundance, just waiting for the encouragement of one good reader to reveal itself.

The reader creates the writer. The reader creates the relationship that makes it worth writing. To write is to risk; it has to be worth the risk. It always is worth the risk when you know someone has received your communication, shared some of your experience and read your work with a sympathetic imagination. It obviously is not worth it if they treat your hard-won words casually – even if they are full of benign praise, routine lazy comments like 'V.G.' or 'Well done'.

A PART

These poems
are like
a diary.
Understand them,
you won't,
forget them
you will.
But it's a part of me.

Tony Nelson (16)

Tony expresses his fears about the reader's ability and willingness to receive him, but defiantly asserts that his writing is vital to him, and, in spite of the apparently depressed resignation of his statement, that his reader is vital to him too. These two

34

TEACHING THROUGH POETRY

contradictory assertions succeed in making the unspoken plea
('Understand me, don't forget me, read me with care') reverberate
in the reader's mind. The title puns on the tension.

This chapter is about two aspects of the teacher's role in the
drafting process: the teacher as the responsive audience creating
an encouraging environment (the 'good reader'); and the teacher
as a critic of the craft, advising on effective structures and
techniques. The second aspect, critical tutoring, is illustrated
with several examples in the section, 'How to Tutor a Child's
Draft.'

The Good Reader

The teacher/reader must read pupils' writing with concentrated
attention and *make the following assumptions in order to make them
come true*.

— Assume that each word and phrase has meaning and expresses
  the writer. Therefore, if parts of the writing seem garbled or
  irrelevant you do not put it down to stupidity or flightiness,
  shake your head and smile; you ask what they were trying to
  get at, and tease it out. You will make remarkable discoveries.
— Assume that each phrase can communicate with you and
  requires sympathetic and imaginative concentration.
— Assume that pupils may need help and time to clarify their
  meaning and discover it fully, but that they are *not* just
  wittering away to fill paper.

These assumptions serve to create an atmosphere of trust and
respect and show pupils that we have high expectations of each
sentence. The assumptions will come true as the writer responds
to the standards set by the reader.

Marking

Marking is one of the few opportunities for most teachers, busy
with classes of 30 pupils, to give full attention to individuals and
to offer them personal tutoring. A heavy timetable and other
duties can make marking an unwelcome intrusion on the teacher's
private time after a full day's work. Casual, resentful or flippant
marking undermines the rest of the writing programme, whereas
constructive and specific comments on drafts matter more than

anything else. If you respond to pupils' work making the above assumptions, in a period of a few weeks the assumptions will bear fruit.

Marking has three elements, which must not be confounded. The first is the activity which is the subject of this book: responding critically and constructively to drafts, questioning what is unclear, stretching pupils by suggesting lines of future development, commenting on the direction, shape and coherence of the text, and giving enthusiastic encouragement, urging pupils to their top level of achievement. We shall call this the *tutoring* function of marking.

The second element of marking is *proof-reading and the detection of errors*. One great advantage of adopting a drafting policy for your teaching is that you separate these two aspects: proof-reading becomes important not to you, the teacher, but to the pupil whose work is going to be presented in public. Naturally the writer wants to present the work with its face scrubbed and its best clothes on. At this point you can help with errors; but, better still, you can seize the moment of high motivation to raise the whole issue of *how to detect your own errors and where to find guidance on them*. Good spellers and dab hands with the comma briefly become high-status members of the class, valued for their ability to help their colleagues. Dictionaries actually get used. Questions are asked about grammar and punctuation. This is the crucial last stage in the drafting process, and it is your opportunity to teach all the technical skills of the literate presentation of writing. It does not take long either: pupils want an answer *now* to a particular technical problem and so are eager and quick to absorb information. If they have *characteristic* errors they will diagnose this themselves – 'I always do that, don't I!' You can remind them to take care next time, and give special praise when they have learned to control this aspect of language.

The third element in marking is *assessment*. What you are doing all the time in the course of commenting on drafts in your *tutoring* (element one) is holding a dialogue with pupils on the quality of what they do, so there should be no need for assessment in the sense of informing pupils of the standard they have reached, except with the older ones who need to have a clear idea of where they stand in relation to GCSE criteria. However, you will need to take stock every now and again for your markbook, school record sheets, the headteacher, and parents.

When marking creative work which is part of a programme of writing following the sort of aims outlined here, i.e. is intended to develop awareness and problem-solving skills, and transferable personal skills, the criteria for assessment are more than a judgement of achieved quality. They reflect the aims and reward *assiduity, improvement,* and *problem-solving linguistic skills* as well as quality.

We must not confuse assessment with the other two aspects of marking and undermine the tutorial function. Assessment must come, if it is required at all, at the very end of the drafting process, when the writing is in its final state. Alison, Una and Louise, Andy, Lee and Lee and other children whose work is quoted below would all have to be assessed as having failed lamentably if their first attempts were judged. If we assess work before it has had a chance to grow into its mature self through the drafting process, we manufacture failure, we 'de-educate'. There is no such thing as an 'unimaginative class' that 'cannot do creative writing', in spite of what some teachers will tell you. If we show pupils that we can read, they will show us that they can write.

The good reader reads with care, and performs the tutoring function on drafts, giving an honest and generous response according to the assumptions outlined above. This is more important than flashy 'stimuli', lots of bright ideas, being a popular personality, having a degree in English, loving all the children, or knowing all about 'elaborated' and 'restricted' linguistic 'codes', not that each of these things is not excellent in its way. Readers make writers. Anyone taking care and applying their judgement sensitively can be a good reader. But the long-term aim is, of course, to teach the class by example how to be good readers, thinking as skilled practitioners of the art, reading critically but non-aggressively the work of their peers; and, soon after that, how to read the work of all writers in the same spirit.

Performance and publication

The writer's next best motivator, after finding one good reader, is to find a lot more. The teacher can arrange for young writers to reach a wider audience through *publication*. Finding an audience introduces the delight of sharing, gives the writing official status, brings useful feedback into the drafting process and even brings some local fame.

There are many ways to publish in schools. At the simplest and cheapest level you can read out pupils' writing in class. Build on this by reading to visitors, or to another invited class or to larger school and community audiences. More elaborate performances can be prepared, in which sound effects and/or music are added, or choral speaking is arranged or dramatisations both serious and comic are used to interpret the poems. When the flow of writing is established you will be ready to offer a selection to the local radio station.

Individual bound book covers for each pupil can be made. Class magazines are best, however, because they reach an audience beyond the classroom, and because each pupil has a copy to keep which includes other pupils' writing as well as their own. Do not wait for the once-yearly glossy school magazine with only enough space for six poems. Get your publishing done quickly, with every pupil's work represented. In the early motivating phase, use a typewriter at least once, even if in the end you decide that publishing poems in the children's own handwriting is your preferred policy. The typed page looks like print. To pupils, it may be the first time it has ever occurred to them that their own blotched scrawls could attain the dignity and authority of print. For those who badly need to see themselves transformed from Cinders to Princess or Frog to Prince, time spent correcting spellings and typing up a poem smartly, centred on the page, with space all around, works a miraculous metamorphosis.

How to Tutor a Pupil's Draft

The second aspect of the teacher/reader's role is advising on the crafting of poems and songs. There are two kinds of skill a teacher needs to read a pupil's draft poem and facilitate the drafting process.

The first is non-specialist, something that most teachers, not just English specialists, should be able to do well. It is to detect the phoney and recognise the real. All it requires is close attention to the reading, and common sense human judgement. Ernest Hemingway said that the most important piece of equipment a writer needs is 'a cast iron shit detector'. The teacher of writing needs one too, to nose out the false, to pinpoint the parts of a

poem which have gone dead. You need to read like a wheel-
tapper, testing each phrase for soundness. The positive aspect
of this capacity is detecting and encouraging true observation
and feeling. An insecure pupil, conscious of failure, shows you
a scruffy sheet of paper. The handwriting is a mess, there is a
scatter of irrelevancies and false starts, but you are able to draw
from it a theme that has been buried under the uncertainty and
encourage it to stand up, dust itself down, and step forward into
the light. In the process of encouraging pupils to recognise which
things are sound and which things are superficial, you are
teaching the most fundamental and valuable kind of thinking:
the sensitive but concentrated application of one's judgement to
a creative project, the sifting of ideas until the essential subject
is revealed. Getting the words right is the only way to clarify
ideas and is the fundamental task of education. William Blake
put it with characteristic force when he commented on painting:
'Without Minute Neatness of Execution The Sublime cannot
Exist! Grandeur of Ideas is founded on Precision of Ideas.'

The second kind of skill required in reading a pupil's draft is
more specialised: it is a matter of thinking in terms of poetic
craft, and is developed by reading and trying to write poetry.
One must have a view of how the medium can lift and strengthen
expression. With more formalised kinds of writing, such as the
songs and metrical verses discussed later in this chapter, this
awareness takes on greater importance. We shall start with
examples of tutoring the severe difficulties of the least confident
writers.

For the least able pupils, all the stages of learning they have
to go through in order to achieve a patterned form need explicit
teaching. Choosing a subject can be a difficult process in itself,
but even when that is decided, the slow learners have a major
problem with visualising *how it might be turned into a poem or
song*. This problem is made up of four specific difficulties, any
one of which could abort the enterprise. First, they have great
difficulty in seeing the potential of the subject. Secondly, their
awareness of forms and structures is limited. They have as much
experience of nursery rhymes, jingles, playground chants and
pop music as anybody else, but have not 'disembedded' the
structural features of these, and have difficulty in thinking of
structure as distinct from the whole rhyme and its meaning.
Thirdly, they have difficulty in imagining the end-product – how
could their subject ever make a song? Fourthly, unless they have

been very lucky in their schooling, they may be inured to failure and find it difficult to conceive of themselves as persons who could take an active and successful part in writing a song and entertaining an audience. The following example illustrates the problem.

Andy, Lee and Lee are 10 and 11 year olds, identified by the school as needing extra help with literacy. Having chosen to write about BMX bikes they could not apparently see much farther than this (these are their first notes):

> Some BMXs are light and heavy
>
> off the ramp he drops in with his Skyway Wheels with his bike he corners
>
> black helmet   pads on the clothes

By the time I saw them they were dispirited and thought that their subject was no good and nor was any other subject. They needed a teacher's encouragement to see the opportunities afforded them – all the drama, the glamour of the machinery, the competitiveness, the display of skill, and their own expertise with the special BMX jargon – and to have faith that it could make a successful piece of writing.

Their second difficulty was that they were unable to imagine how they could shape a scatter of observations into a structure similar to those we had discussed when we had listened to pop songs earlier. We had listened to a song about surfing, and love songs, but these structures seemed remote achievements that they could not relate to themselves. At this stage we did not have other songs by their classmates, which would have provided better examples. Here the pupils are in a Catch 22 situation: they cannot see how they can do something until they have done it and have no way of doing it until they can see how to do it. There are ways of pushing on to the next stage in the process, however. The principle of organisation for their 'BMX' fragments could be a narrative one. They could tell a story about a BMX race or accident. This could be the simplest and most accessible way to get the elements to cohere. At their level of development it would be asking too much to expect them to organise on a thematic or conceptual principle. Alternatively, they could use the rhythmic structure of song to organise their fragments. They would need help to define such a structure and also source material to select from. I did not consciously choose this latter

course, but as they told me about BMX biking I saw the potential
of the specialist vocabulary which they were explaining to me.
They warmed to the subject and baffled me with as many weird
and wonderful phrases as they could. I suggested they just list
as many of the esoteric terms as possible. This is the list they
made:

                    rollback
                    bunny hop
                    kick turn
                    alternator
                    drop in
                    one hand one foot wheely
                    flipper
                    revolution
                    Haro master freestyler
                    lay back
                    Skyways
                    GT performer
                    four point two revolution
                    180 aerial
                    360 aerial
                    cherry picker
                    wheely hop
                    kangaroo hops
                    bleeper
                    hop back
                    white and black Mags
                    Pro-mag burner
                    area seat

This was promising raw material but the pupils had to be led on
to the next task. They were asked to tap out a rhythm to fit a
tune they knew, or a newly made-up tune. I helped them, when
I returned, to write this down so that they could refer to it. It
went:

                    dum dum dum
                    dum dum dum
                    dum dum dum dum dum

                    dum-dum dum-dum dum-dum dum
                    dum-dum dum-dum dum-dum dum

They were now having to analyse structure and many doubts
appeared as they tapped and recorded. It took time to recognise

the features of pattern, and separate the repeating line units out from the whole. We were nearly there, though Andy, Lee and Lee were still unsure where they were going and not believing they could get there anyway. With their tune and rhythm firmly fixed in their minds, they had to fit words from their list into the sound patterns, take decisions about which combinations pleased them best, and which to repeat for a refrain. This is a matching task, essentially, like those intelligence test items using spheres, cubes and pyramids of three colours, only this one requires aural matching and effective strings of items in combination. Best of all, it results in a product to be proud of. It is not the same kind of mental activity that produced the poem 'Methuselah' quoted in Chapter 1, but a problem-solving puzzle which offers opportunities for exercising flair in the selection and combinatioin of words. This is their completed work:

BMX

BMX
BMX
Up the quarter pipe
    Flipper, lay back, wheely, hop
    Revo-lution off the top

Cherry picker
Cherry picker
One hand one foot wheely
    Flipper, lay back, wheely, hop
    Revo-lution off the top

Bunny hop
Bunny hop
BMX kick turn
    Flipper, lay back, wheely, hop
    Revo-lution off the top

Aerial cowboy
On his bike
Up the stunt ramp tricks
    Flipper, lay back, wheely, hop
    Revo-lution off the top

    Andy, Lee and Lee (10, 10 and 11)

Set to the tune, accompanied by percussion and a spirited performance, this makes a good song. Although it is not in our terms a particularly sophisticated piece of writing, for these boys this represents real progress in manipulative skills, and a significant social success that gave them a sense of pride and satisfaction. They ended up where they never conceived that they could be: members of that élite caste one sees on *Top Of The Pops*, singer-songwriters. Words were used here almost as arbitrary rhythmic units, but because they also have meanings we have a much more interesting combination of elements than those you get in a 'culture free' cognitive task like the matching activities of IQ tests. Lifted by the tradition of song which the pupils are now enrolled in, their manipulation of words as rhythmic units becomes a celebration of their chosen activity, and a score for a rousing performance involving voices and movement.

Finding the theme

The next example also concerns pupils who have difficulty in seeing the way in which their subject can develop, and who have little sensitivity to the rhythmic and formal opportunities of song structure. Once again, their first effort, if judged as a completed task, would have to be called a failure, but here we are treating it as a tool for thinking with and using it as a means of extending their sense of competence.

The introduction to this task was to listen to and discuss songs with a question-and-answer structure. We looked at the border ballads 'Lord Randal' and 'Edward Edward' and the American song 'Cotton Eyed Joe' in a version sung by Josh White. It was suggested that the pupils use the question and answer structure like an interrogation. There would be a mystery and the awful secret would only be revealed at the end.

JANE WHERE HAVE YOU BEEN?

Jane where have you been?
Jane where have you been?
I've been to London to visit the Queen mother
How did you get there?
By a bus.
What with money of course
but where did you get the money from through the post.
Dad why are you asking me all these questions?

Una and Louise (9 and 10)

Una and Louise made a desultory start, borrowing the nursery rhyme questions and answers for the first four lines, but without any apparent sense of direction, and by line seven still did not seem to have any idea what their theme could be. They ran out of steam and ground to a halt. When I came to see how they were getting on, I was rather dismayed by their lack of progress, and the lack of anything much to build on. I asked what the reference to money was all about and they said the mother had sent it. That sounded more promising. Somewhere in this embryonic story was a tense conflict between father and mother, with Jane caught in the middle. I told them it was (as specified in my introduction to the task) mysterious, and I wanted to know how it would work out. I wrote a quick memo to them on the script to focus their attention if they lost their way again: 'This is getting more interesting, with the fear or suspicion of the last line. Carry on now until we find out *why* he *is* asking these questions.' The next stage of the draft, when I returned, continued:

> Because I want to know questions
> Are there any more questions
> Yes (there is
> WHAT?)
> Why did you go to (and see) your mother?
> Because I haven't seen my mother for a long time
> What did your mother say.
> That I could stay with her.
> What did you say to that
> I said I will live with mother.

We had certainly got the theme clear now! The writing grows in confidence in the last five lines, after the hesitant start, and gathers pace, driven on by the awful logic of the father's fears. The lines assume a much more authoritative voice and use strong direct phrasing. The pupils now needed to have their attention drawn back to the structural specifications: alternating questions and answers in pairs; and evenly matched line lengths. I left them to solve these technical problems. Now that they could see it as a whole and knew where it was going, it wasn't too difficult.

JANE JANE WHERE HAVE YOU BEEN?

Jane Jane where have you been?
I've been to visit mother

But where did you get the money from?
Through the post that mother sent me

Dad why are you asking these questions?
Because I want to know questions

Are there any more questions?
Yes, why did you go to see mother?

Because I haven't seen her for a long time
What did your mother say?

She said that I could stay with her
And what did you say to that?

I said I will live with Mother
I said I will live with Mother.

                                                    Una and Louise

This needed a little more polishing (the 'Because I want to know questions' line is odd and the rhythms are rather inelegant, especially in the first half), but Una and Louise successfully used the interrogation structure to uncover a disturbing secret and their song ended with a ringing assertion.

This seems to be an example of a writing task that became a channel for significant articulation of feeling. The song structure has enabled a sense of conflict and divided loyalties to be expressed, and an emotional 'decision' to be announced (for all we know, it may have been a personally important admission for one of the young authors). The song is protected by convention from being taken as personally revealing, however, and the writing can proceed in a non-threatening context in which everyone is content to admire the formal successes in the use of the medium.

Una and Louise's song is an example, like Alison's later in this chapter, and Andy, Lee and Lee's, of a successfully completed task wrought from initial failure. I have no doubt at all that children in these impasses are abandoned daily to failure in our schools, when a teacher could easily rescue them and help them gain the blessings of achievement.

Finding the shape

We shall now consider a difficulty that confronts more confident and ambitious writers. Iain's draft below, shows that although pupils may have quite a good ear for rhythm, and be able to write a complex and tuneful stanza, they may be unable to analyse and reproduce the structure for subsequent stanzas. Pupils have to learn, as they work with forms, that rhythmic patterns must be, above all, consistent. Whatever pattern you start with, you must sustain (the only exception is when you deliberately break the pattern to disrupt readers' expectations, e.g. for bathos). The opening lines of a poem create the conventions by which it is read. If you are not rhyming, avoid at all costs introducing one rhyme in the middle, however tempting. Stick to the rules your opening lines establish.

FALCONS

Streaking like an arrow through the sky
See the Falcon madly rushing by
Catching food, for all her brood
Hear them screech and cry.

Perching on the cliff, seeking out its prey
Hear the other birds say, 'Look out it's
  the Falcon!'
Then they all begin to pray.

Iain Howard (12)

Iain was encouraged to identify the structure of his first stanza: two long lines and a shorter fourth line, all rhyming together, and a third line made up of two short sections, internally rhyming on a different sound. It only took a minute of my time to establish this with him. He realised that the second stanza was a disappointment after this highly patterned start and immediately set about reconstructing it.

FALCONS

Streaking like an arrow through the sky
See the Falcon madly rushing by
Catching food, for all her brood
Hear them screech and cry.

Hear the small birds screech with fright
The falcon will catch them alright
Catching food, for all her brood
She returns to the nest for the night.

Delighted with his new sense of control, Iain used the stanza again:

BARN OWL

The owl drifts slowly through the wood
I only wish that I could
Like a snowflake, falling on a lake
It takes the mouse like it always should.

Drifting slowly through the night
It could give you quite a fright
Like a snowflake, falling on a lake
It floats off into the night.

Iain was a bird buff, as you will have guessed.

Finding a voice

Our next example of how to respond to pupils' draft scripts is very different and does not represent a 'problem' at all. Darren, who is 12 and does not have any of the learning difficulties of the 'BMX' or 'Jane Jane' authors, wrote a poem:

EAGLE

The eagle sits perched high on the mountain top
It sees everything that happens below.

A movement way down beneath him,
In a flash he is swooping down. . .
. . . down he goes helped by his strong wings

A screech and the eagle's claws
Lock on his prey,
Up up he flies back on his perch
High on the mountain top

                              Darren Loveday (12)

The eagle is described from an observer's point of view, as a natural history film or book might represent it, but with special effects to heighten the drama of the dive. It is a perfectly satisfactory piece of writing, with a good circular form, starting and finishing on the mountain top, and a story to tell which illustrates the macho power of this vision of the eagle. The most vivid sense of power comes from the line, 'It sees everything that happens below'. Reading this, I felt that Darren was imaginatively identifying with the eagle and it brought to mind Ted Hughes'

'Hawk Roosting'. I could not lay my hands on the poem immediately to show Darren, which was probably just as well as it would have pre-empted Darren's treatment of the subject. I simply suggested to Darren that he might find he could express the eagle's sense of power more effectively if he tried another poem, this time written from the eagle's point of view.

THE EAGLE'S WORDS

I the eagle king of all
I the king both strong and tall

I swoop I screech
I grab I kill
Every bird obeys my will

When I the Eagle flies in the light
Every small bird gets a fright

When I screech
It means I'm mad
When I'm calm small birds are glad

I claw my way
Into a mouse
I the Eagle am a power house.

The third section, or stanza, still needed reworking (or perhaps to be cut altogether); Darren seemed to have slipped half back into the third person viewpoint again, and 'gets a fright' is one of those tired old formulations that provides a simple rhyme without convincing the reader that there is any energy in the observation. Also, although the poem had an extremely powerful couplet structure, with four emphatically resonant beats to the line, Darren had not yet quite recognised in visual terms what his rhythmic pattern was, nor made up his mind how best to represent it on the page. That said, Darren's words give us a pretty remarkable assertion of the eagle's power – as amoral, brutal, uncompromising, unashamed, gloating, and pleased with its own physical strut and swagger as Hughes' hawk itself is.

Finding awareness

Overleaf is a draft of an intended song. The original became scruffier as it went on, the handwriting more spidery, almost self-mocking in the last two lines, which I took to be a sign of ebbing confidence:

> When I'm feeling down
> I walk over to your
> I tell you all my troubles
> Your   Someone to share them with
> It makes me happy.
> I put on Madness
> and that's fine for me
> I think of Suggs and break my mug
> and that's the end of it.

Alison (10) was depressed and had run out of steam. She was bored and fiddling with her pencil case. She was urged to do a bit more and added:

> I turn on Duran Duran
> and listen to reflex
> and then It Makes me happy
> I sing away.

Here she ground completely to a halt, and when she got an opportunity to speak to me, expressed her frustration. She thought the poem was a failure; she thought she couldn't do it; she had written 'rubbish' and was 'no good at writing'. It is certainly true that her piece of writing had lost all sense of direction, had deteriorated from a promising start, and was suffering from disorder. This arose from the confusion of two tasks I had set which were intended to be kept separate. The first focused on moods and on how one copes with them. I proposed a structure which began 'When I'm feeling. . .' and went on to describe what one did in response (we discussed this theme); the second was concerned with the effect of music on one's mood and began, 'When I hear. . .' or 'When I'm . . . music makes me. . .' (we had listened to Chuck Berry's 'Rock and Roll Music' and Otis Redding's 'Sad Song'). Alison's confusion arose from the fact that she was trying to do both tasks at once and was falling between two stools. There was no reason for incorporating her favourite group, Madness, and their singer, 'Suggs', into the poem and therefore lack-lustre lines, degenerating into feeble and pointless rhyming ('Suggs' and 'mug'), ensued. Adding more lines, this time about Duran Duran, had not improved matters.

How would you have responded? Would you have let her fail at this task and hoped that she did better at the next one? That would have been the thing to do had there been nothing on

which to build, but in this case there was a good subject for
development.

I spoke briefly to Alison and told her I found the opening lines
interesting: who was she writing about? She told me it was her
aunt, the most sympathetic listener she knew and the person she
turned to in times of trouble. I asked her to read the first five
lines aloud to me and we agreed that they had a satisfying
rhythmic pattern – a four-line group and a last line which Alison
thought of as a chorus. I suggested she told me more about her
aunt and tried to do so in a four-line stanza matching the first
four lines she had written. At no time did I mention the lines
that had failed; we just focused on the theme of her relationship
with her aunt. Our conversation only took two minutes and this
sort of tutoring *is* possible in classes of 30 children, while writing
is in progress. This is her draft of a second section:

> Then I sit down
> and relax
>   I listen to you
> Like you listen
> to me
> I'm happy to talk
> that's fine for me

Alison was still not feeling successful, however. She knew her
subject was real and clear but doubted whether she could do it
justice. As she came to a halt this time, all she needed was an
encouraging word: 'Yes, you are getting there; just shape it into
four lines that will "match" the first four, i.e. will eventually fit
the same tune.' She gained a new surge of confidence and very
quickly finished her song.

The only change that was made subsequently was to elaborate
the chorus, which at this stage was still 'It makes me happy'.
This developed naturally in the course of creating the tune.
Alison improvised the repeats in the chorus to shape it to fit a
four-line musical pattern. When Alison started work on the
music, with a colleague of mine, Sean Sweeney (a music specialist), we discovered that she had a good singing voice, which was
a lucky bonus. The tune she wrote was very simple. She said
she did not know what to do with the first line. Sean said try it
on one note, which she did. He said, 'Up or down for the second
line?' and she sang it going down and returning to the tonic.
'Why not see if the third and fourth lines fit the same tune, and

see if you like it?' said Sean; they did, and she did. 'Should the
chorus line about being happy go up or down?' Up. She climbed
the scale in her pure tones and then returned to the tonic again
for the newly-developed phrase 'Happy to share them with you'
on the one note. I have a recording of her singing it to Sean's
accompaniment, and it is beautiful.

> When I'm feeling down
> I walk over to you
> I tell you all my troubles
> You're someone to share them with
>> It makes me happy, happy
>> Happy to share them with you
>> It makes me happy, happy
>> Happy to share them with you
>
> When I'm all fed up
> I sit down and relax
> I listen to you, listen
> I'm happy to talk, that's fine
>> It makes me happy, happy,
>> Happy to share them with you
>> It makes me happy, happy
>> Happy to share them with you

Alison O'Callaghan

It is not, of course, a brilliant poem – that is not the point. It was
a satisfying achievement for Alison, when she thought she must
fail. It is also an example of what I mean by teaching *through*
poetry. She learned about her own capacity to *think*. She had
problems – she lost her focus on the subject, and had difficulty
sustaining the formal pattern – but she solved them. She overcame
doubts and failures, proved to herself that she could take control
of her writing and, incidentally, learned some of the 'wrinkles'
of a craft. What is more, she had classmates come up to her and
ask her who she was singing about and tell her they thought it
was a really good song. She experienced the great social blessing
of communication, enabled by the tradition of song, and will
know next time she sits down to write that it is possible for her
to share her feelings with others.

This is more than saying that language allows one to talk to
others. It is the strongly-made, formally-patterned, publicly-
performed properties of song that make her communication
about her aunt more than a piece of information, of passing

interest only to her close friends, as it would be in conversation. Shaping the statement has, I am sure, brought her appreciation of her aunt sharply into focus.

Borrowing the cultural prestige of poetry and song to make elegant and emphatic statements, quite literally increases *awareness*. To develop *awareness* is a major aim of education, as we saw in the last chapter. There are two separate kinds of *awareness* involved in the process illustrated by Alison's song. First, there is the awareness of her feeling for her aunt, which became something palpable for her as she articulated it; it separated itself from her and became available for *thinking about*. One starts *thinking about* a subject when one realises that there is a choice of two words and one weighs up which of them will best define it. 'We heighten our awareness of what is actual by considering what is possible' is how Margaret Donaldson summarises some research studies into self-awareness by Piaget. Once one has defined the feeling one can apply all the thinking processes because the definition (or song, in this case) is now an independent, self-contained text. One can analyse it, doubt it, meditate on it, judge it, or use it as a complete *idea*.

The second kind of *awareness* is the sense of control over language that comes from organising the words not for meaning alone but for pattern. Margaret Donaldson's thesis is that children who do not succeed at the intellectual tasks of schooling need to be shown how to practise 'disembedded' thinking: 'What is going to be required for success in our educational system is that [the child] should learn to turn language and thought in upon themselves . . . the first step is the step of conceptualising language – becoming aware of it as a separate structure, freeing it from its embeddedness in events' (Donaldson, 1978). She is referring here to the awareness of words that comes with early literacy. At a higher level, the process Alison went through, of isolating her real subject, choosing to emphasise the word 'listen' by repeating it, and shaping her idea into the song form so that the second stanza led naturally to the refrain, is a disembedding of the language, a conscious mastering of the organisation of words.

A word about the teacher's role in tutoring the drafting process: in making comments about Alison's draft I was not telling her how to write a song, according to a fixed formula. My comments were designed to help her to see the potential of her subject and the implications of her form. I did not create her song but I was its midwife. It would have been still-born if there had not been somebody in attendance who did not panic when faced with a song-writing crisis.

Through writing you can make half-conscious perceptions take shape in front of you, open to scrutiny, in a way that may seem curiously brazen, though you wrote them yourself. Awareness comes to pupils by making free-standing objects of their vague, doubting notions.

PART TWO

The Writing Programme

4 Mucking About in Words

Introduction

This chapter, and the four that follow it, outline a writing programme that is intended to erode pupils' resistance to poetry and to establish the writing and reading of poetry as core components of an English (or language) curriculum. Ideally, however, these chapters should be read in conjunction with the two chapters of Part Three ('The Writing Process') which discuss the writing journal and the writers' workshop, both features of the writing programme. While it would be inappropriate to attempt to establish either the journal or the workshop before the work outlined in Chapter 5, you may introduce either at any stage thereafter.

Getting the Flow

In any British classroom you are likely to be faced with some children for whom writing has been associated from the very beginning with a sense of failure and humiliation. They feel that the English language belongs to the 'disembodied worthies' who compile textbooks and comprehension cards, and that their own clumsy attempts to put words on paper are invariably 'wrong'. They have lost the consciousness that they possess their own language and can flourish it arrogantly, juggle with it entertainingly, declaim it earnestly, insinuate it teasingly, or fence with it furiously. It is hardly surprising: their own language is neglected and they spend an inordinate amount of time copying the 'Coco-Pops language' of school books into their project folders or exercise books. Coco-Pops language is a product made by adults for children, with everything already done for them (sugar and cocoa flavour added). All the nutty husks, the bits that might need chewing or stick in their teeth have been carefully removed, leaving behind a bland, well-meaning discourse, which is the register of the informative books published for schools, and of far too many of the language textbooks.

The first stage with a class that lacks confidence in expressive writing, is to encourage the pupils to feel that they can experiment with language, break the rules, be inventive, play with words, and gain a confident sense of control over the medium. If their language is in a sickly condition, then the teacher may need to take them back to the play stage, to 'give them permission' to be frivolous, inventive and stylish, and to take risks, with a devil-may-care sense of fun.

The *sine qua non* for a successful writing course is to get a flow of writing underway. Then you can build up confidence, rate of production, and commitment, until pupils are secure enough to respond well to criticism.

Publication, and having a good reader, are the fundamental long-term motivators as we have already seen, but there are other strategies that help in the short term. At the beginning of the writing programme, especially with demoralised and suspicious pupils, 'getting the flow' is done by a campaign of pump-priming motivation – an assault on all fronts. Even the most obstinate will find it hard to resist! The four approaches below concern pump-priming in the early stages.

1   You start with games and formulae with which even the least confident can have some success (see pp. 57–61) and praise extravagantly every minor achievement. The praise at this stage can be uncritical and unearned (though you use your judgement, of course, to decide who is confident enough to be treated critically and who needs larding with encouragement). The more dependent pupils will just enjoy it; the more independent ones may well feel that you are a soft touch for rewarding handsomely sub-standard writing that only took them a few minutes to complete. You are laying the foundations, however, because while showing delight at their work and dishing out rewards you are also asking what they meant by 'X', letting them know that you read with the expectation that each phrase will really say what it means.

2   To reward pupils, use whatever lies to hand. Shower them with gold stars, house points, rounds of applause in assembly,

a note to a parent, or whatever they respond to in your school. If they are in a state of readiness to appreciate the gesture, give them poems. Do not hand out a duplicated copy of something to everyone, to be left on the floor or lost in the playground, but make it clear that these are selected gifts, to be treasured. With younger pupils the prospect of making their own books is exciting and all can value their own folders in which to keep favourite pieces.

3   Sheer enthusiastic salesmanship works well. Give lots of verbal reassurance; promise them all the nonsense that advertisers promise – *poetry will change your life, writing will boost your thinking power, communication skills will improve your relationships* – you have as much right to use these myths as anyone else.

4   Communicate enthusiasm through short poetry readings. Mix the writing of established poets with the writing of children in these readings. If possible, get writers from a class of older pupils who have already tasted success to come in and talk about their writing, show their magazines around and sing their songs.

The games, formulae and exercises below are designed to provide opportunities for mucking about in words. They are the first part of the writing programme, leading after a short while into the group poem (which models the drafting process) and the development of individual free writing through the writers' workshop approach. Do not spend too long on these games and formulae. Make a selection, get the flow of writing going, and then move on to the group poem.

Word Games and Nonsense

Amongst the word games that can help to release inventive sharing of the fun in a language lesson are:

1   **Yes, No, Black, White** Pupils fire questions at the person in the hot seat and they must answer without using the four proscribed words. If they are too good at it you can vary the rules and introduce other taboo words. The pupil whose question makes them slip up is next in the hot seat. This is a battle of wits demanding ingenuity in questioning and resourceful circumlocution in answering.

2 **Call My Bluff**   This is an inventive dictionary game played
   by teams. It can be adapted from the well-known television
   model and based on school dictionaries, but it is that much
   more exotic if you have access to a really meaty dictionary
   full of strange and archaic words, complete with etymologies
   and histories of usage.

3 **The Furniture Game**   Sandy Brownjohn describes this
   delightful game in *Does It Have To Rhyme?* A pupil invents
   metaphors for a character, prompted by the others in the
   class asking questions in order to try and guess who the
   subject is, such as, 'What kind of furniture is he/she? What
   kind of vegetable? Vehicle? Fish? Weather? Building? Bird?
   Animal? etc.' (The game works just as well the other way
   round, with the class sending one person out of the room
   and agreeing their subject, then the returning one asking
   questions while all those in the class develop the metaphors.)
   In the same book, Sandy Brownjohn also describes other
   suitable games: the old surrealist game **The Exquisite Corpse**
   (a kind of *Consequences*); **Adverbs** (acting actions in such a
   way that others can guess the adverb); **Lexicon Sentences**
   (a card game using a Lexicon pack); **Telegrams**; **Questions
   and Answers** (pupils answer each other's questions, swapping
   papers in pairs); **Preferences** (alternating lines of 'I love X
   because . . . ' and 'I hate X because . . . '); and **Prepositions**
   (writing lines starting with different prepositions – behind,
   under, next to, etc.). Sandy Brownjohn describes more games
   in her second book *What Rhymes With Secret?* and has
   published two books of word games called *Word Games* and
   More Word Games. See also *The Gamester's Handbook* by
   Donna Brandes for drama games and interaction exercises.

4 **Inventing a Language**   A role play exercise in which a cave
   man and a cave woman meet a million years BC. The class
   can all take part in pairs, or you can seat the class in a circle
   round a cleared space and watch two of the extroverts, all
   sharing the fun as an audience. Having no language, the
   prehistoric couple try to communicate by inventing words
   for things and teaching them to each other by pointing,
   miming and gesturing. Apart from being a great opportunity
   for comic inventiveness and laughter, this exercise is very
   instructive about parts of speech. Pupils discover that nouns
   are the first necessity, and that having named some things,

they need verbs. They may need prepositions too, but adjectives, adverbs and the grammatical items are later refinements they can well do without. They are also much less easy to explain by acting or pointing!

5 **Pass the Story On** This is simply telling a story around the room. There are several possible variations of the rules: you can have a 'buck', an object (pen, shoe, ruler or whatever) that is passed or thrown from person to person, and whoever receives it has to continue the story (in chunks of defined size); or you can sit in a circle and each person has to say one word in turn, quickly, passing the story around; or you can build in infuriating subversions of the story by having two teams facing each other, and when the first person of one team has started with a statement, the next one from the other team has to begin with 'but . . . ' and undermine it, the next continuing by trying to re-establish the story, and so on.

6 **Words Found In An Envelope** A filler activity for those who have finished early. Prepare some collections of vocabulary items: nouns, verbs, adjectives, and adverbs (the pupils are allowed to add in their own grammatical link words and alter case number and tense to suit their purposes) and put them on separate cards in an envelope. The collection should not have too many words, say between 15 and 25, and they can be quite unconnected (for greater absurdity) or loosely related to a subject theme. A word may be used more than once. The pupil constructs a poem using only the words found in the envelope.

Here are examples by girls of 10 at Meadowlands Middle School, Hampshire:

THE OLD WAYS

Fire and flames are high remembered
When smoke and spirit shone black
When thorny hills cloaked the sun
And time was old and ancient
Embers whispered in the fire
Stones were crooked,
Cinders lay evil,
And still the ancient fires burnt.

Claire Leate

Ancient black evil shone
high over the sky and whispered
to the flames and smoke,
soared past time's embers
black and ancient from the fire
long ago.

Linda Brown

The restrictions imposed by the limited vocabulary forced creative problem solving on the pupils, and encouraged them to some fine phrase-making: high remembered; shone black; thorny hills cloaked the sun; stones were crooked; cinders lay evil; black evil shone; time's embers.

7 **Surreal Cut-up Poems**   I have not tried this with younger children, but it is fun for teenagers who are already aware of the obscurity of some poetry. They are delighted to find that they can make the meaningless sound meaningful, and fool their friends with it. Each person in a group makes up a line of a poem without consulting the others and writes it out on a strip of paper (two lines each if it is a small group). If they agree a theme or common mood in advance it gives the finished product a more convincing and coherent air. Then they shuffle the lines into a random order and write them out as a poem, tinkering here and there to make subjects and verbs agree and furnish conjunctions or punctuation to link up the unconnected lines. The following was composed by four 14 year old CSE class girls in a few minutes and they managed to impress some of their colleagues with its profundity before revealing that it was randomly written. They relineated the draft.

Lonely and by himself
He's in a world
Of his own
    Rejected
    Ugly
    Confused
Blue thoughts –
World of fuzz

> Afraid
> Ultimate in sausages
> Blew his mind.
>
> Wendy Poppleton,
> Anita Norbury, Jane
> Lilley and Sandra
> Firth (all aged 14)

An entertaining spin-off of this frivolous exercise was that they sat for ten minutes with serious faces justifying the significance of 'ultimate in sausages' to doubting friends, developing an imaginative line of convincing gobbledegook.

8 **Invented Words and Nonsense**   Humour in English is rich in inspired nonsense: Lewis Carroll, Edward Lear, John Lennon, Roger McGough, Spike Milligan, Dame Edna Everage, scripts for and books based on *Monty Python*, *Not The Nine O'Clock News* and *The Young Ones*. For the very young there is the nonsensical charm of nursery rhymes. This is all good material to liberate in pupils a feeling of power over language. They can do what they like with it, and take a holiday from the demands of making sense. Still the best starting point for invented words is Lewis Carroll's 'Jabberwocky' which can lead to extraordinary artwork, drama or dance; this form of verse can also lead to 'cod' definitions and daft dictionaries, or to new poems/stories on the same model with new-minted words, like this:

SEA

> The latey sea upon the ficcs
> Slagey upon th ejaley srook
>
> Crashing sliff, dashing sliff
> Oh, the mighty bashing sliff
> (etc.)
>
> Susan Hoaksey (11)

In this case it diminishes the impact to tie down the new words to definitions afterwards, and they are best left alone, as Carroll left his.

Some advertising campaigns can suggest ways of being inventive. Advertisers have given us many new coinages, from the raunchy zest of 'finger-licking good' to the sinister 'understains'.

Collections and Lists

Collect and relish categories of language. You can simply collect
and enjoy talking about them, or develop them into list poems.
The possibilities are endless. Make collections of clichés, politicians' euphemisms, advertisers' boasts, pretentious and blunt
words, foreign words, slang phrases, dialect words, 'feminine'
and 'masculine' words (rich pickings here for those with a nose
for the absurdity of stereotypes), proverbs, onomatopoeic words,
words-I-like and words-I-dislike, 'U' words and 'Non-U' words,
tautological phrases, family catchphrases, eavesdropping treas-
ures (snatches of language overheard on the bus or at family
gatherings), funny-sounding words (remember Neil Simon's
assertion in *The Sunshine Boys* that words with a 'k' in are funny:
'*Ls* are not funny. *Ms* are not funny. Tomato is not funny;
lettuce is not funny. Cucumber is funny.'), 'poetic' phrases and
'unpoetic' ones, soft and hard words, passionate and unromantic
words, fundamentally untrustworthy words (start with Orwell's
political examples like 'resettlement', 'liquidate', and then go
into the special idiom of school rules, assemblies, young lovers'
promises), double-edged or ironic words, etc.

Many of these categories lend themselves to playing with the
language through drama: explore all the wonderful range of
language styles of different regions, ethnic groups, classes,
occupations, personality types and family situations. Have pupils
act out short sketches that exemplify embarrassment, blustering,
evasiveness, wheedling, boasting, hypocrisy, vanity, foolishness
and all the other staples of comic entertainment through the
ages. Needless to say, this kind of 'mucking about in words'
increases children's auditory discrimination, critical sharpness,
social awareness and confident deployment of a wider range of
linguistic registers.

The list makes a good simple poetic form and has been the
basis of many successful poems and songs, from the mediaeval
lyric 'Death' (Stone, trans., 1964):

> When my eyes are fogged
> And my ears are clogged
> And my nose turns cold
> And my tongue's back rolled
> And my cheeks slacken
> And my lips blacken
> And my mouth blubbers

And my spittle slobbers
And my hair stands up
And my heart-beats droop
And my hands quiver
And my feet stiffen –
All too late, all too late,
When the bier is at the gate!

Then I shall go
From bed to floor,
From floor to shroud,
From shroud to bier,
From bier to pit
And be shut in it.

There lies my house upon my nose
And all my care for this world goes.

to Michael Rosen's 'Chivvy' (a good subject for classroom imitation) (McGough and Rosen, 1979):

Grownups say things like:
Speak up.
Don't talk with your mouth full
Don't stare
Don't point
Don't pick your nose
Sit up
Say please, etc

Another good topic for imitation is Ian Dury's top ten hit song, 'Reasons To Be Cheerful' (see Chapter 6 for classwork on the obverse, 'Reasons To Be Miserable'):

Reasons to be cheerful part three
One two three

The juice of the carrot, the smile of the parrot,
A little drop of Claret, anything that rocks,

Elvis and Scotty, the days when I ain't spotty,
Sitting on the potty, curing smallpox . . .
etc.

The basic list has the advantage, as a form for writing, that each item is more or less equivalent, and the order does not matter (logically, that is: it might do if you are rhyming, as Ian Dury is, or for rhythmic purposes). More highly-wrought list poems can be developed which build up items in a sequence to a climax,

but in its simple form a list poem is undemanding. Because the
convention of a list is already established in the mind of the
reader, no further explanation is necessary and a bare list can be
a satisfying whole, complete in itself. Apart from selections from
the collectable categories of language, the teacher can suggest:
shopping lists that reveal character; collections of rhyming words,
or words with the same vowel sound, or starting with the same
consonant cluster; lists of similes, superlatives, exaggerations,
alliterations.

Here is a fanciful list of collective nouns, by a lower stream
11 year old playing this language game with robust assurance
and taking it beyond the task set to conjure a landscape of
powerful symbols:

THINGS

Mountains of sorrow
Valleys of fire
Woods of blood
Meadows of cries
Dales of spirits
Countrysides of ghosts
Depths of sorrow
Curtains of guilt
Heart of gold
Bundles of pleasure.

Kerry

The starting point for this following list is the girl's initials:

W. G.

White gale
weather guide
warm gloves
wet garden
winter gardens
water games
welsh gig
wonderful girl
wine grove
wide groove
worn grass
watery grave.

Because it is based on her name, it has the potential for symbolic meaning to be attached to these phrases and for the poem list to become charmingly expressive. I have seen the work of 8 year olds following this idea, beautifully displayed with elaborately decorated initial letters. All the poems had a personal freshness that was very satisfying.

Formula Poems

These derive from ideas found in Kenneth Koch's book, *Wishes, Lies and Dreams* (Koch, 1980). Koch tried out a number of subjects with middle school pupils in New York, and came to the conclusion that the most successful themes were 'Wishes', 'Lies' and 'Dreams'. The examples I quote below come from English schools, but Koch includes an anthology of children's work in his book that provides more source material. The best way to start children writing formulae is simply to quote from the work of other children. They very soon pick up the idea. Then you can take it as far as you want to in discussion with the writers and devise more complex or penetrating formulae.

'Lies' is a subject that, like nonsense, gives the writer freedom to cast off the work-ethic obligation to be serious. It can also provide an opportunity for expressing a truth without being held accountable for it!

LIES

My house is made of mushrooms
My chairs are made of toadstools
My bed is made of shortcake
My pillow is made of gingercake
My fridge is made of jelly
My mum and dad are made of paper
My cooker is made of fire
My tables are made of ice cream
and I am made of Christmas cake.

Angela Collings (11)

The line about 'mum and dad' sticks out like a sore thumb and clearly symbolises some real perception in contrast to the delightful edibles that fill the world of the poem, but we have no right under this title to take it seriously.

'Dreams', like 'Wishes', can be simple lists, or some alternating

pattern along the lines of 'I dreamt . . . /But really . . .'. It is
also a fine subject to develop at a non-formulaic and more
sophisticated level. Another variation of the theme is to construct
a dream house, line by line, according to the formula, 'In my
dream house there are/Floors of . . ./Windows of . . . ' etc.
Here is a further variation developed by a hostile and unhappy
boy, a frustrated low achiever at school, whom I encouraged to
write about his anger when I saw that the 'Dreams' subject left
him cold:

> In my angry room there are
> Windows of broken glass
> Tables of rage
> Bed of fire
> Carpet of blood
> Cupboard of rubbish
> A brass bed knob of dents
> Pillow of cuts
>
> Philip (11)

Of the other formulae that Kenneth Koch developed, a consistently successful one is, 'I used to be . . ./But now . . . ', or 'I
was . . ./But now . . . '. The following example shows how a
formula works. It differs from the Ronald Ridout style of
formulaic language instruction in that the gaps in a Koch formula
are genuinely open and each pupil is helped by the formula to
reach a unique expression. The formula essentially provides a
simply balanced form. Even the least able can succeed, completing four or six lines, and have a strongly shaped work, complete
in itself and expressive of the author. This may be, for the poor
writer, the first wholly successful achievement in writing. Then
it can become, through publication, an occasion for receiving
praise and for feeling proud. Stephen was a bottom-stream 11
year old:

> I was a sea-otter but now I'm a seal
> I was a tiger but now I'm a cat
> I was an emperor but now I'm a tramp
> I was brainy but now I'm dumb
> I was king but now I'm evil
> I was sweet but now I'm bitter
> I was the beginning but now I'm
> The End.
>
> Stephen

In the first two lines he is being fanciful and playing a fairly meaningless game with the formula, though perhaps the second line is the beginning of the idea he perceives, as he realises there is potential for him in the theme of contrasts that the formula shapes for him. By the third line meaning has come sharply into focus and nothing can stop him developing a stinging series of images for his experience of failure and disappointment, ending with a stylish and wry little flourish.

An evergreen joke thrown up by this formula:

> I used to be nice to teachers
> But now I'm cured.

> Matthew Close (12)

The range of possible formulae is endless. Some good ideas are, 'Pronoun . . . Who . . . ' poems; 'Why . . . Because . . . ' poems; 'I seem . . . But really . . . ' poems; and poems with lines for each colour of the spectrum. Koch has some good results with a mystical idea, 'The Third Eye', in which the lines of the formula poem describe things that the visionary third eye can see that the ordinary organs of perception cannot.

What follows is an account of three different inventive extentions of one formula, and how you can devise formulae of your own for particular topics, according to your classroom needs.

Julie Scarborough, a Portsmouth First School class teacher, took the idea of 'Inside . . . / Outside . . . ' as a simple formula, and developed these two ingenious variations with children in her class. She brought a pomegranate to school one day, and without giving its name, talked with the pupils about its appearance. They wrote the 'Outside' section. Then she cut it open, they tasted it, she gave them the exotic name, and they wrote again about the inside. Amanda Spencer (7) wrote this:

MYSTERY FRUIT

> Outside its
> Round like a yellow
> Apple smooth skinned
> Onion shaped
> Mini-pumpkin-shaped
> Yellowish orange
> Chocolate brown spots and bruises
> Like an apple with a
> Mini-sized chimney

An apple with a
Funny chimney nose.

POMEGRANATE

But inside its like
Red jelly with
Cream in pips like seeds
Red fire with orange flames
Tomato insides
With crimson pips
Memories of melons
Boats on a sea of jelly
Blood red bird seeds
Red paint with white blobs.

In another exercise the pupils drew and coloured faces, cut out the paper in silhouettes and wrote on the faces the 'Outside' and 'Inside' of a character. The 'Outside' piece of paper was then clipped on top of the other so that the 'Inside' was revealed by folding it back. Linda (7) drew a pretty, blonde, smiling girl on top and a scowling creature with a scar underneath:

THE YOUNG GIRL

Outside she is
Beautiful. She has long
Golden hair with cheeks
Like pink roses and eyes
As blue as the sky
And skin like a golden
Peach. She has lovely
Long eye lashes.

But inside she
Is ugly and as
Nasty as a witch
And wanting other
People's things. She is mean
And she is horrid.

Ewan Proctor, a Portsmouth middle school teacher, encouraged his pupils to see the opportunities for using the same formula for thinking about themselves:

INSIDE OUTSIDE

Outside I understand something difficult,

Inside I know that too much is expected of me,
Outside I feel confident and positive,
Inside there is always that little bit of doubt,
Outside when I'm faced with danger I'm eleven,
Inside I'm a small timid baby,
Outside I feel hurt and sick,
Wondering why? But sometimes I don't have to wonder.
Outside I sometimes let go of my feelings and cry,
Inside I feel a lot better.

Gary Woodward (11)

Formulae allow you to split up the writing task into short bursts, suitable for those with a short concentration span. If a sustained piece of writing is the goal, it can be built up from several formulae sequenced and edited together. Introduce each formula with 'Conversations' to help pupils talk their way imaginatively into the subject with a partner and you will create a varied lesson of short bursts of concentration. You can offer conversation topics at different levels of ability. For example, on the subject of 'Death', following on the telling of an old ghost story, I offered a straightforward narrative conversation to the less able: 'You have "died" during an operation and been revived. Tell your friend the story of what you experienced'; and more demanding tasks to more advanced pupils: 'A psychologist tries to give a rational and reassuring explanation to someone who swears that their house is haunted', and 'A religious person gives advice to a sick friend on how to die well'. Imaginations warmed by conversations, the pupils can then write. When designing formulae, use the patterns of *alternation*, *contrast*, *sequence* and *climax*, and focus attention on *the five senses*.

At the moment of death I feel anger
A minute after death I feel grief
An hour after death I feel tense
A day after death I feel free
A week after death I feel safe
A month after death I feel relaxed
A year after death I feel mad
Ten years after death I feel normal
A hundred years after death I feel close again.

Garry Wiltshire (12)

Now I have died
I can see a different land

I can hear a rumble in the distance
I can feel soft hay underneath me
I can smell a spring meadow
I can taste the strong taste of strawberries.

Zoe Pettinger (11)

Angles of Perception and Shape Poems

We value highly observant writing that brings into focus part of our recognisable experience. One way of sparking off a fresh look at the familiar is to choose a device that alters the angle of vision: a zoom lens moving from long-shot to close-up; a slow-motion description of a simple action; a worm's eye view or a bird's eye view; giving a voice to an object; looking through magnifying glasses or microscopes. Here is a slow-motion description, a record of impressively caring, accurate observation, by a CSE stream 14 year old:

CUTTING PAPER

The piece of paper's long
and thin,
the scissors are sharp,
they cut precisely and
they cut clean,
the line is straight no
bends or curves.

My fingers and thumb
pressure the pivots and
the scissors slice.
The action is up
down and forward.
The screw in the middle
needs oiling and the
tool screams with use.

As I nearly have finished
my task,
my hands are tiring.
This job's very boring
and takes no skill.
When the job's over I
pull my finger and thumb

from the holes.
I've been sweating and a
red ring marks where I
held the scissors.

Paul Gosling

Literature celebrates the world by making us look at it more closely, by depicting some neglected corner of it with loving attention. It is not enough simply to tell your audience that they cannot see and order them to look again, as Yoko Ono did by cutting a hole in a piece of canvas and calling it 'Painting to Look at the Sky Through'; the artist communicates something of the intensity of his or her own quality of looking. 'My Hands' was written by a 13 year old after looking at his hands through a magnifying glass. He was supposed to be looking at dead insects, stones, moss and tree bark, but turned the instrument in fascination on his own hand. The advice given was to try to see the subject as an environment for creatures on a different scale from ourselves and imagine what it would be like to travel through the landscape. He starts with close description, then peoples the landscape and imagines adventures.

MY HANDS

The baked parched soil of my skin,
With intricately patterned furrows, rushing streams
    and patchwork grids,
The field of minute plants swaying under the breeze
    of my breath,
My hands pitted through endless toil,
The pores, shell-craters in the battle of the hands,
The skin everywhere, snake-like renewing itself.

At the end of the finger,
An endless pink ocean with small white boats adrift
    on it.
A white cliff to climb before the skin is reached,
The cliffs above the sea pitted
With the grapnels of warriors advancing to the top.

Small pouches of skin, old men with double chins,
Talking about the good old days of the war,
And grumbling about the new generation,
It was not like that when I was a boy, they chorus.

The little finger, a beautiful maiden,

Not without her faults, not pure, but small and
seemingly defenceless.

The spaces, sanctuaries between my fingers,
hiding those that are falsely accused.

Richard West (14)

Sandy Brownjohn, in *What Rhymes With Secret?*, recommends
another perception-enhancing exercise: staring. 'The idea is to
stare at something for a long time and to jot down all the pictures
you begin to see. The sorts of things which lend themselves to
this are a blank area of wall, a single brick, a puddle, a piece of
bark, a square of earth or grass, . . . a marble, . . . a dark
corner, and so the list can go on.' Desk tops, with historical
layers of carvings about love and the quirks of teachers, make
good subjects too.

The potential for the effective display of poems as shapes is
already well understood by teachers – the snake poem that
slithers across the page, the bonfire poem with lines leaping as
flames – but all sorts of inventive layouts can be devised that
help one to see the subject afresh. A boy drew two faces in profile
and wrote about how two people failed to communicate in the
space between them. Copying ideas from concrete poets (the
source I use is *An Anthology of Concrete Poetry* edited by Emmett
Williams), pupils make figures built up of appropriate character
words, with rain words descending to obscure them; or have
battles between opposed sets of words that merge and tangle; or
represent a word graphically. ('Silence' is a concrete poem by the
Swiss poet Eugen Gomringer which is composed of a block of
typing of the word 'silence' with an empty space in the middle.)
Alphabetical letters of different sizes and typefaces can also be
cut from newspapers or magazines to construct pictures.

There are many ways of writing out the lines to represent the
subject, but 'My Cupboard' is an ingenious variation: the opening
and closing sections are arranged in an orderly poetic structure.
By contrast, the jumble of the cupboard is not so much 'pictured'
as represented in terms of the medium of lines of verse (see
illustration (a) opposite). In the same class of 13 year olds, Anna
Boniface devoted hours to finding a graphic form in which to
represent the meaning of each word in her poem about a pebble
from the beach. It makes the poem difficult to read but represents
a sustained exploration of a creative strategy by Anna, in which

My Cupboard

My cupboard is a dark tan,
The handles are polished brass,
The grain moves in random patterns,
Glossed and slick with varnish,
Although the outside is scratchless,
The inside is a confusing tangle.

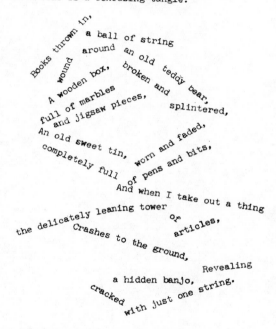

Books thrown in, a ball of string
wound around an old teddy bear,
A wooden box, broken and
full of marbles splintered,
and jigsaw pieces,
An old sweet tin, worn and faded,
completely full of pens and bits,
And when I take out a thing
the delicately leaning tower of articles,
Crashes to the ground,
Revealing
a hidden banjo,
cracked with just one string.

Objects bringing back memories
Of early childhood, of a
cut, freckled-faced child.

I pile the games back in to cover
The memories.

What a mess, my cupboard.

                    R. Voysey

illustration (a)

Anna Boniface.

illustration (b)

she devises some inventive solutions (see illustration (b)).

The main aims in the early 'mucking about in words' phase of the writing programme are to have fun and to build up confidence. In the course of doing the exercises pupils also pick up valuable experience. From the formulae they learn the strength of simple structures. They are given permission to be eccentric, nonsensical, humorous and to do unconventional things with words. They detect from clues the teacher's attitude towards their writing. And they should see their work in print, reaching an audience. This is a good foundation. You move on from the play stage as soon as confidence is high and pupils are gaining amusement and satisfaction from writing. The serious writing starts with the group poem, described in the next chapter. The group poem models the drafting process; it is the beginning of learning how to select and order words to represent experience.

5 The Group Poem

The group poem is the best starting point for more assured, non-formulaic writing. Its advantages are that it models the drafting process clearly, shows what can be done and how to approach it and effectively sweeps away misconceptions. The priority is to engage pupils in writing and convince them that they can succeed at it and find great satisfaction in sharing it. When they know that and have internalised the process modelled here they will have lost their misconceptions about poetry without a word having been spoken on the subject.

Group writing has five phases: the class members share a common experience, preferably a physical one; a board is covered with notes, everyone volunteering phrases, with the teacher drawing out alternatives and improvements; on another board the poem is constructed by voting on favoured phrases and lines from the notes; the fourth phase is lineation – choosing where to break the lines and how to set the writing out on the page; the fifth and most important phase is the individual writing that pupils do subsequently. All five phases are described more fully later in the chapter.

The group poem works with all ages but is a lot faster and more productive (in quantity) with unsophisticated groups. Intelligent pupils over 13 or 14 with a critical training and some literary experience are highly self-conscious about their language. They find it very difficult to produce more in an hour's discussion than a few ungainly lines, hiding behind an arch pose of irony. They have to be reintroduced to direct observation, reporting of scientific precision, and should only be allowed to build up to the use of imagery step by step.

No such inhibitions dam up the flow of ideas for 6 and 7 year olds. 'A Walk In The Woods' (below) is a group poem completed in an hour (the writing that is – the walk took a hour as well) by

pupils from a Hampshire infant school. It is full of vivid
similes and drives confidently forward.

A WALK IN THE WOODS

The sound of boots in the mud is like sucking
the last of a drink with a straw
and the sound of the long-tailed tit is like a siren.
The pond water is like custard
and the mud at the edge is like chocolate yoghurt.
We saw the water boatmen
like bouncing bombs skidding across the water's skin
on ice skates. Moving like swervy subs
under the cling-film skin of the water
Gonzo the curved-nosed shrimp darts.

Hart Plain First (7/8 year olds)

The Shared Experience

The group poem takes at least an hour to produce, not counting
the experience it is based on. The ideal arrangement is to set
aside the whole morning, take the class out in the first session,
and return with an hour and a quarter remaining in which to do
the group writing before lunch. The class will write as a group
and must therefore have some common experience to write about.
The best kind of experience is a physical one. I have taken classes
out for walks, and drawn children's attention to the view and
the colours, only to discover that what excited *them* was charging
down the hill in the five minutes free running around time I
allowed them at the end.

PRIMROSE HILL

You could see a fantastic view of London Town
And you feel free and cool and big
Because of the fresh Breeze on your face
And the tiny Buildings all Grammed and
Bundley up together far off below you.
You sprint down the Deep Hill
Feeling all Loose as though
Taking off into the cool air;
You feel Shaky all over
As your feet tingle at each pace
Nervous in case you slip

The Sound of boots in the mud is like Sucking the last of a drink with a straw and the sound of the long-tailed tit is like a siren

The pond Water is like custard and the mud at the edge is like chocolate yoghurt We saw the water bootmen like bouncing bombs skidding across the water's skin on ice skates. Moving like swervy subs undar the cling-film skin of the water Gonzo the curved-nosed shrimp darts.

As the buildings stride up bigger and bigger.
You drop into the leaves weak and dizzy
Relieved, but Sad because you're back to normal
Under the huge blocks of London Town.

Class 1H (11 year olds)

I now plan some physical exertion as part of the walk – what better subject for vivid descriptive writing could you have than 'a stitch', or exhaustion?

AT MILTON PARK

At the Park there was a warmish breeze
And when I looked up at the bright sky
My eyes watered.
The high wintry clouds looked like smoothy-spread
Mashed potato.
When I went for a run my heart drummed
Like horses' hooves,
And when I stopped I had an agonising stitch
As if I had been stuck by a dart.
My throat was dry
And I collapsed on a seat.

Meon Middle School, Portsmouth (8 year olds)

Walks in cemetaries make good subjects; so do council rubbish tips; boiler rooms and churches (places with a distinct atmosphere you can feel with your senses); and markets, big railway stations, ferries, etc. But if, as in some secondary schools, your timetable absolutely prevents you from organising such a visit, then you can arrange to have a common physical experience in school: plan to do the writing immediately after a PE lesson, swimming, or dance. Or start the class with arm-wrestling, press-ups, or racing round the playground. Alternatively, you can provide some unusual subject in the classroom: a pound of whitebait from the fishmonger's so that each child can examine a fish closely; or sheep's eyes (free, but order a few days in advance) from the butcher's, which you can dissect. Another subject I tried when I had no time to take a class out was 'Your Head'. We talked and wrote notes as we went through a series of explorations: rolling the head to feel its weight and the stretch of the neck muscles; feeling with fingertips the bones, eye-sockets tendons and muscles of the skull, jaw and teeth; knocking on the bone and stretching the skin; finding the pulse in the temple and neck and listening for the blood rhythm; feeling the nose, snorting the air, sniffing out smells and so on with lips, tongue, vocal chords, ears and throat. The experience that caught their attention most, that they chose to write about, was deep breathing (don't do it fast – it could be dangerous).

The group poem that resulted was not very successful as a piece of writing to excite a reader, but it was highly successful in its primary purpose, which was to show the pupils the process of writing. It does not matter whether your finished group poem is a good poem or not if it succeeds in starting the flow of confident writing from the class. This is the piece of writing that emerged on the subject of heads:

> When I stop to think
> I hear jungle drums beating in my head sending
> confused impulses in syncopated rhythms as
> the blood mingles with the steady heaving of my lungs.

It is very short and incomplete. The class were bright and sophisticated 13 year olds and were already suffering self-consciousness about language. They worried over each word and argued, never satisfied that the language matched their experience. They worked very hard debating these few phrases for an hour. But look below at what this piece trawled up in its wake! A boy came in with 'ME' the following week and good writing flowed thick and fast from the class.

ME

> When I stop to think,
> Beneath my skull lie complicated
> Rhythms as my blood mingles with the tide of my breath,
> It seems that there is a well tuned engine
> Purring somewhere inside,
> Keeping me going,
> Ticking over,
> Humming thoughtfully as it digests the data of the world
>   around me.
> The armour-plated skull only seems to
> Resonate the sound.
> It is the boss of me.
> 'Big Brother' in fact, which sometimes reigns tyrannically
>   over me.
> I am possessed with thoughts which grip my being,
> But why!

It is just me,
Pondering over matters.
My brain is one vast computer, controlling every twitch
    of my muscles.
Every want or desire.
It has a vast memory bank which I can delve into at will.
Keeping it tidy,
Well informed,
Groomed,
Reading for action.
My body has its own thermometer,
Gyroscope,
Etc,
I am a gigantic machine,
Built like a fortress,
But with a delicate, minute, accurate system inside.
My jaws, primarily used for preparing food for the tortures
    beyond
Can also communicate
So articulately and freely,
With such a large range of sounds that one can only
    wonder at it in awe.
Can, in an instant be armed with a two edged sword
Which can break down other 'fortresses'.
Whoever would believe that two marbles can have
A projector each;
A screen each;
And a curtain each;
With regular refreshments on hand,
Which work as a perfect team
Constantly giving film shows to my brain,
All of these things are many years old,
But are still just as good as new,
Irreplaceably minute,
Protected in a humble bone casing.

Andrew Wright (13)

On the walk, or while going through the common experience, there is no need to make notes, but it is worthwhile to talk about the experiences and probe with questions to sharpen the articulation. For example, a child comes up to you after running round the park and flops down on the bench saying, 'I feel shattered!' You try and get them to define the 'shattered' state with great precision: Where do you feel it? In your chest, your legs, your head? Is it a dull pain, a sharp pain, a rhythmic pain?

A red feeling, a yellow feeling, or a black feeling? Is it like being squeezed in a vice, or like floating, or like having a fever? Is 'shattered' a good metaphor for it, or is it more like being wrung out, or just born, or what? But the walk/visit itself can be a fairly relaxed affair; the real hard work of sharpening articulation is done in the first half hour of the writing process, back in the classroom.

Notemaking

Once you have decided on your subject and arranged for the class to have a common experience of it, you prepare the room. You need two large blackboards, or overhead projectors, or one of each, and you need the class to be sitting together, not spread out around separate tables. They must be brought together, preferably all sitting at the front in a semi-circle.

When you are settled in the room you immediately start filling the first board with notes. Start with anything the pupils volunteer, anything they noticed. The aim is to go beyond the first superficial descriptions and draw from them many alternative phrases to describe each item.

The teacher has to put a lot of energy into the class writing, sustaining concentration and the involvement of all pupils by enthusiastic leadership, communicating growing excitement as they explore the subject and start contributing more vivid and imaginative phrases under the pressure of the teacher's probing questions. To take an example: the group of 8 year olds working on 'At Milton Park' quoted above, was trying to describe the sky. 'Cloudy' was suggested and duly written on the board. 'What kind of clouds were they? Big, low puffy ones?' 'No, high up clouds.' This was added to the board notes. 'Like cotton wool,' someone else said, which was added to the notes, and another interpolated, 'They were sort of spread out.' Asking them not to let go of this idea and to think of comparisons to the texture and form of the clouds brought, 'Like margarine'. There was a laugh of pleasure at this and it was added to the board notes. 'We have got "like cotton wool" and "like margarine"; did they remind you of any other things?' Pause. 'Like a lamb's back' (added to the board). 'Like mashed potato' (added to the board). 'What about their movements?' and so on. The final line as it emerged after the second part of this process described below, was,

> The high wintry clouds looked like smoothly-spread
> Mashed potato.

which was a combination of a number of ideas contributed by
different pupils. With a rich choice of phrases to draw upon,
they rejected the trite comparisons with cotton wool and a lamb's
back in favour of the striking and accurate simile of spread out
mashed potato. None of this would have been achieved if the
first easy formulation – 'Cloudy' – which they were quite willing
to accept, had been seen as sufficient. No better definition of the
subject English has yet been given than that it is concerned
with 'the best words in the best order', to borrow Coleridge's
description of poetry (*Table Talk*, 12 July, 1827). Group writing
is work at the cutting edge of language where each word
is weighed and tested for soundness, examined for signs of
preciousness or dishonesty and then its place is found in the
order.

To guide you in the phrase-forging activity, bear in mind the
principles informing the writing process:

(a)   reach beyond the obvious, beyond the first easy formulation;

(b)   strive for absolute accuracy, 'Was the sky really blue? Look
      out of the window now', and for precision, 'Where do you
      feel it? High in the chest, or down here? Deep inside, or
      spread over the surface?' – you are teaching them that there
      is a most important premium value set on close and careful
      observation and on honest recording;

(c)   use the multi-sensory approach, 'What did it smell like?
      Did any of you put your hand into the mud? What did it
      feel like on the skin? What sounds did you hear?'

(d)   when appropriate, make sparing use of the figure of speech
      that describes one sense in terms of another (synaesthesia), to
      solve problems of description (especially where vocabulary is
      limited, as with smells), 'Yes, I know it is difficult to find
      the words to describe smells – could you describe this smell
      in terms of a place, a colour, or a feeling?'

(e)   ask for comparisons, to generate the exciting metaphoric
      connections that are the imaginative element in writing;
      and

(f)   encourage plain unpretentious language.

Pretentiousness is an issue that may or may not arise explicitly in the course of the lesson but it is an important part of the sweeping away of misconceptions. Your emphasis on accuracy and honesty of recording observations will make the point effectively, but it will give the class a golden opportunity to debate the issue if, for example, one pupil has guessed that what you are doing is a 'poem' and volunteers ambitiously 'poetic' phrases. You write them on the board of notes, along with the other offerings and then when the voting and choosing starts the pupils have to make up their minds whether the March breeze they felt is more accurately and honestly recreated by the phrase 'the rippling of a balmy zephyr' or by the observation that, 'the chill breeze tickled the little hairs on my forearm'. This kind of choice, which arises continually because of the nature of the exercise, is where the real learning takes place: the pupils control their language; they can choose to be flamboyant and eloquent for a particular purpose, if it suits the mood and style of the piece; or they can choose to be plain and clear. Discussing their choice, they come to appreciate the special quality of each style, that they have more than one style available to them and that they can bring their decision making under conscious control.

Composing

After half an hour of filling one board with alternative descriptive phrases, you stop. You will not have covered all aspects of your subject, but you will have enough to write from and you must allow time to compose. You now move to the second board and ask for suggestions as to where to start – 'Give me a first line'. This goes on the board with any alternative suggestions and the alternatives to particular parts of the phrase, taken from the first board of notes, are listed. The simplest way is to colour code the choices on the first board. Then the pupils vote for a particular adjective, or for whole phrases. The class may not be happy with the result and may make further suggestions for combining the chosen adjective with one of the outvoted words to form a new phrase.

You move forward by consensus, by listing choices to vote on, by suggesting ways of turning a sentence around if it is becoming a problem or asking for problem-solving ideas from the class. You refer back to the first board for ideas, but as the writing proceeds you may need to introduce some new phrases.

The process teaches you as much about democracy as it does about poetry! In one infant class I was surprised by the way all the boys voted in a block without considering the qualities of words, until I realised they were all looking to a leader. He chose a word, gave a signal and they all voted, determined to 'win' the vote for their gang. In other cases, pupils who are genuinely excited about a certain phrase and get outvoted can feel frustrated, and the final version is, obviously, a compromise, a committee poem that does not quite please all those who had clear ideas of their own. Some pupils use voting competitively to frustrate their rivals. Clearly, if you can encourage them to use voting for its proper purpose – to express a considered judgement on the words and phrases listed – the exercise will be more valuable. If any are dissatisfied with the group choices they can write their own individual poems on the subject afterwards.

Lineation

Ten minutes from the end of the lesson you must finish the writing and round off the last sentence, because you have two further things to do. The first is to lineate the writing and decide on its graphic layout. You will be pressed for time, so if you can arrange to see the class again briefly after lunch or break the same day to do this, then you can have a little longer to complete the writing, but don't let it go cold overnight. Once again, the lineating is done by offering choices, discussing the merits of each means of presentation, and voting. For example, to take 'Primrose Hill', you could lay it out to give a special boosting emphasis to key words:

> You could see a
> FANTASTIC
> view of London Town
> and you feel
>
>   free
>
>
> and
> cool
>   and BIG
> because of the fresh breeze on your face

and the tiny buildings
all grammed and bundley up together

far off . . .
            below you . . .   etc.

This has a lively visual impact and a pleasing sense of play, but
is so broken up that it makes it difficult to read the piece smoothly
and picture it whole in your mind. It has perhaps too much of
the strident flashiness of the hard sell to be suitable for this
subject.

Alternatively you could decide to use short lines, building up
the impact phrase by phrase, as in this example (you might
decide to drop the 'ands'):

You could see
a fantastic view
of London Town.
And you feel
free
cool
big
because
of the fresh breeze
on your face
and the tiny buildings
all grammed and
bundley up together
far off
below you   etc.

Reading this aloud you will hear that it has a very different effect
from the long-line version on which the class in fact decided. It
has a jerky, cumulative rhythm that might be suitable for
representing danger, showing the process of thinking step by
step, or could be used to good effect to slow the reader down
and make him or her attend to each detail, but it does not
enhance this subject. Class 1H decided to use the most straightforward form of presentation for 'Primrose Hill' and have long lines
corresponding to the natural sense units and the breathing pauses
of speech. This disrupts the flow of the language much less but
still leaves room for some muted special effects, such as the
placing of 'Taking off' at the beginning of a new line to give it
that little extra lift that comes from splitting the phrase 'as

though taking off' over a line (page 77).

Two short poems illustrate how effectively the short-line broken rhythm can be used for a special purpose. Blake's 'The Fly' is baffling to many readers but the silly, singsong rhythm is the clue to how to read it:

THE FLY

Little fly,
Thy summer's play
My thoughtless hand
Has brushed away.

Am not I
A fly like thee?
Or art not thou
A man like me?

For I dance,
And drink, and sing
Till some blind hand
Shall brush my wing.

If thought is life
And strength and breath,
And the want
Of thought is death;

Then am I
A happy fly,
If I live
Or if I die.

This is a comic satire on a certain kind of small-minded logical thinking. The premises and proofs are stitched together in a buzzing zigzag of complacent philosophising and lead to an appropriately half-baked conclusion.

Jacques Prévert, translated here by Lawrence Ferlinghetti, takes what in prose would be unremarkable and by using short lines charges it with intense suspense and suffering.

BREAKFAST

He put the coffee
In the cup
He put the milk
In the cup of coffee
He put the sugar

In the *café au lait*
With the coffee spoon
He stirred
He drank the *café au lait*
And he set down the cup
Without a word to me
He lit
A cigarette
He made smoke-rings
With the smoke
He put the ashes
In the ash-tray
Without a word to me
Without a look at me
He got up
He put
His hat upon his head
He put his raincoat on
Because it was raining
And he left
In the rain
Without a word
Without a look at me
And I took
My head in my hand
And I cried.

As the poem unfolds you realise that a woman is speaking and that the short lines of unwavering observation represent her anxious search for a sign, but only amount to a halting catalogue of banalities.

The 'natural' long line is the length of a phrase or breath unit and is the basis of most English verse from Chaucer through Shakespeare to the present day. Extra-long lines remind us of Biblical rhythms. They are well suited to prophetic and apocalyptic subjects and to building up an incantatory rhythm for lists representing an all-embracing vision, as in Christopher Smart's much-anthologised 'My Cat Jeoffry', Blake's prophetic books, and the work of the Americans, Walt Whitman and Allen Ginsberg.

In ten minutes at the end of an exhausting morning on the group poem, there isn't time to explore the issue of line-length in detail. If you are teaching the class the same afternoon you could allow yourself a more leisurely look at lineation and rhythm then, but on no account leave it overnight before finishing. What you can do in ten minutes is to write out quickly three or four alternative versions of the first sentence or two to demonstrate the effect of different line lengths on the manner of reading aloud. Give one long-line version matching natural sense units, one short-line version, and one or two versions that use more surprising effects – alternations of long lines and single word lines, or ambitious graphic effects using huge capitals for certain words and exaggerated spacing for others, or a drawn 'frame' appropriate to the theme.

The class has to listen to the effect of each on the ear when read aloud, and consider the strengths and drawbacks of each style in relation to their subject, before voting for a strategy. Then it is simply a matter of going through the draft on the board, putting in alternative coloured strokes for line endings at places they suggest, and numbering them for voting purposes. Your group poem is now finished. A smartly written version is needed as soon as possible, on display.

The pay-off of the whole session comes in the last minute: you just have time to enthuse over the class's achievement and set them the immediate homework of writing a poem that evening. It must be on a subject that the pupils can observe closely and apparently dull topics can be very good: a blade of grass; an egg; having a bath (many will still get on better with a physical experience); a pencil; toast and marmalade, etc. Absolutely out of the question are such objects as: the leopard; a river from its source to the sea as poetic image of life; any kind of crystal kingdom; any generalised category (my granny's hands, or face, could be an excellent subject, but 'old age' is not).

Average pupils in any class will then be writing poems of this quality, right at the beginning of your writing programme:

MY STREET

Uniformed street
looking sad
a lamp-post
on guard.
Aerials pointing
ready to
FIRE.
A car
drifts away

unwanted.
Washing
swaying in the breeze
like flags
people walking about
as if they are officers
inspecting the
parade.
Everything quiet
except the birds
singing
cheerfully to
themselves.

Malcolm Wheatley (14)

THE EGG

Like a baby in its mother's arms
It nestles in my hand.
I feel the silk-smoothness of its speckled shell
As I turn the slippery oval.
Then Splat!

It drops to the floor.

Sword-sharp spikes pierce its heart
And yellow blood flows out, mingling
With the clear, slimey liquid into which
Broken shreds of petal-thin membrane
Are curling up, in pain.

Ruth Crook (13)

6 Songwriting Structures

I shall now report on some projects which involved pupils constructing song lyrics. This is 'drafting' in a rather different sense, as it is not so much concerned with responding to children's rough drafts with suggestions to help them improve or develop their writing, but rather with planning activities where two or more stages are required in the development of the complex final structure. Children necessarily *draft*, because editing, re-arranging, selecting, and grafting elements together are built into the task.

The List Song

In Chapter 4 I quoted from Ian Dury's song, 'Reasons To Be Cheerful':

> The juice of the carrot, the smile of the parrot
> A little drop of Claret, anything that rocks

which is essentially a list of his likes arranged in rhythmic patterns with an added refrain:

> Reasons to be cheerful, part three
> One two three

Borrowing this structure to use with a class, the first requirement is a list of observations on a theme of 'Reasons To Be Miserable' . . . or 'Reasons To Be Angry' . . . 'Reasons To Laugh' . . . or 'Reasons To Be Grateful' . . . (they did not take to this last suggestion for some reason). Pupils jot down all the things that occur to them, in any order:

REASONS TO BE MISERABLE . . .

school, boys, family arguments
bad injuries, gym coaches,
sad films, washing up,
horrible gym routines.

                    Vivienne (10)

weather
death
war
animal cruelty
sad songs
losing
divorce

          Michael (9)

With one class, I collected all their lists, reproduced everyone's
phrases on one side of a sheet of paper and took them through
the editing-into-rhythmic-form process as a class exercise, thinking that they would need to be directed by me. This was not in
fact the case; the editing task can be managed by groups of
children on their own at 10 years old, as we shall see.

We established a rhythm by clapping and chanting: two strong
monosyllabic beats, which we just called 'Dum, Dum,' followed
by a quickly skipping phrase with three stressed beats, something
like 'diddle-diddle-diddle'. The class repeated this until it felt
familiar. Then they looked through the phrase collection for
phrases that would fit into their rhythm at any point. It was easy
enough to identify a 'Dum' – 'school', 'boys', 'war', 'death' –
and it was also simple to leap to a phrase like 'horrid gym
routines' and see that it matched the 'diddle-diddle-diddle' part
of the rhythm. As a class, we edited the raw material on the
board:

REASONS TO BE MISERABLE

School, boys, arguing in the family
Teachers, work, and very sad films

Wasps, bees, big black dogs and spiders
Brothers, sisters, bossy mum and dad

Cats, dogs, washing up and drying up
Geography, Maths, and being told off

> War, politics, and cruelty to animals
> Spelling, losing, or when a pet dies
>
> Rain, illness, broken bike and penniless
> Injuries, showers, and horrid gym routines
>
> Snakes, friends, nervousness, divorces
> Death, a wreath, and very sad songs

A little cheating is allowed of course. The scanning of songs is not like the scanning of Greek choral odes or Miltonic blank verse: you can get away with whatever you can cram into the line, and a bar of music can be a bundle of rushing quavers or a single semibreve. We found that extra, unaccented syllables could be carried by the structure, as we chanted and clapped out the words. The refrain

> Reasons to be mis'rable
> Reasons to be mis'rable
> Reasons to be mis'rable
> And to be sad

developed as the class added melody to the lines, with the help of my musical colleague, Sean Sweeney. The tune they came up with was very simple. Line one was chanted on the tonic; line two was a third higher; the first line of the refrain rose to a fifth and the rest of the refrain swept in predictable patterns back to the tonic. They added some accompaniment and sang it with gusto.

In another class I handed over the editing task entirely to the pupils. Working in small groups they succeeded in establishing rhythmic patterns and fitting words to them. They felt a greater sense of involvement in their songs and commitment to them when working in small groups and took great delight in arranging percussion accompaniments and performing the songs (each group gave itself a name, like a pop group):

REASONS TO BE BORED

Washing up, drying up
Doing all the dusting

Sunday, rain
When I'm by myself

Reasons to be bored
Reasons to be bored

Reasons reasons reasons reasons
Reasons to be bored

Hymns, news
Playing with baby brother

Babies   crying
Mummy when she nags

Chorus

Lianne, Sarah, Joan, Deborah and Laura (11)

REASONS TO BE GLAD

Jumps, skips,   clowns and friends
Drawing a picture   that never ends

Happiness it makes me glad
It never makes me feel sad

Balloon, parties,   videos and bubble gum
Hugs and kisses   from my mum

Chorus

Silly faces   from my sister
When my aunt   came up and kissed her!

Chorus

Carol O'Shea (11) and Emily Smith (10)

The songs were then prepared for performance in small groups
and later sung to the school and videotaped. The children gained
great satisfaction from their efforts.

Using Refrains

Una's 'Frog Song' is another example of a piece constructed in
two stages. Initially, Una wrote descriptively about a frog:

The frog jumps with its back legs it looks
With it beady eyes in the night.
Splashing in the water.
The frog goes rabi rabi
[They] She live in the reeds and the weeds, and
long grass.
[They] She feel slimey and slippery.
Splash splash in the water.

Then she worked on the idea of a refrain and had to learn how to get the line lengths to match so that they would be amenable to a song structure. The resulting song lyric is strengthened by its regularity, even line length and use of refrain, and makes a charming piece for performance:

FROG SONG

The frog jumps with its back legs	Rabi rabi
It looks with its beady eyes in the night	Splash splash
Splashing in the water the frog goes	Rabi rabi
She lives in the reeds and the weeds	Rabi rabi
She feels all slimey and slippery	Splash splash
Splash splash in the water	Rabi rabi

Una (9)

Variation in the use of a refrain has also become the organising principle in the revolting dialogue that follows. The different adjective used each time the question is repeated is a source of humour the boys exploit with inventive relish:

WHAT'S THIS. . .

The bell goes for dinner
What's this long stuff?
Be quiet I'm working
What's this round stuff?
Get on with your dinner
What's this horrible stuff?
Shut up you rude boy
What's this green stuff?
Don't insult that dinner
What's this smelly stuff?
Be quiet or else
What's this hard stuff?
Not now lad
Do you call this a DINNER?

D. Paffey (9) and S. Lane (10)

A two-stage composition which started from an idea for a dramatic situation is the next example. The boys concerned always intended it to be a song, and soon hit upon the 'Never! Never!' refrain. They have been quite sophisticated in the use of the refrain: lines lead into it so that it has a different significance six out of the eight times it occurs, a remarkable feat of linguistic ingenuity:

NEVER NEVER

You'd better come down before it's too late
  'Never! Never!'
I'll never come down you better just go away
  'Never! Never!'
We've got you surrounded you might give yourself up
  'Never! Never!'
If you say that again I'll climb on this rail and jump
  'Never! Never!'
What about your wife and kids don't you care about them
  'Never! Never!'
They threw me out just the other day
  'Never! Never!'
You'd better come down you can't stay there all day
  'Never! Never!'
That's why I'll jump you've made your first and last mistake
  'Never! Never!' [*Repeated to four second fade*]

M. Powell, G. Parry and J. Branson (10)

The boys arranged it so that the lines were called out dramatically and the refrain was sung and it worked well as a performance piece. One more brief example is given below of the way a refrain can provide a supporting structure for what is a fairly flimsy idea:

MONEY MONEY MONEY

Let's buy a sailing boat boat boat
  But we haven't any money money money

Let's go to Spain Spain Spain
  But we haven't any money money money

Let's buy a car car car
  But we haven't any money money money

Let's go and have a drink drink drink
  But we haven't any money money money

Carly Harting (10)

Auditory Awareness

Now we come to song structures that are built up through a more complex process, a four-stage development. Before the project started, the class did a series of exercises to raise auditory awareness and encourage them to play with the sounds of words. The first of these exercises was in contrasting rhythms:

> Mini mini mini mini mini mini mini mini
> *PORSCHE!*
>
> Diane Farrugia (11)

> WOOF miaou
> WOOF miaou
> WOOF miaou
> WOOF miaou
> WOOOOOOOOF
> miaouiaou
> WOF
>
> Danny Richards (10)

Teacakes teacakes teacakes teacakes
JELLIES!

Red red red red red red red red
  PURPLE
Black black black black black black black black
  YELLOW

> Sophie Dykes (10)

> Penny penny penny
> Pound penny
> Pound penny
> Pound pound penny
>
> Donna Ryan (11)

The next exercise involved the idea of cumulative or climactic rhythms:

> The rain drops
> On the window sill
> Pitter patter plip plop
> Never stopping still
>
> Sarah Madden (11)

Plane ground   plane bushes
Plane sky   plane clouds
Parachuter out!
Past clouds   past sky
Past bushes   past ground

Clare Jeffries (11)

The third exercise was intended to give rise to aural imagery or
'sounding pictures'. First, I read the class a passage from
Alexander Pope's 'An Essay On Criticism' in which he is giving
advice on verse-writing and exemplifying with consummate skill
how to make lines slow, quick, rough or smooth. I emphasised
that they were to experience the lines with their *ears*:

True ease in writing comes from art, not chance,
As those move easiest who have learn'd to dance.
'Tis not enough no harshness gives offence,
The sound must seem an echo to the sense.
Soft is the strain when Zephyr gently blows,
And the smooth stream in smoother numbers flows;
But when loud surges lash the sounding shore,
The hoarse, rough verse should like the torrent roar.
When Ajax strives some rock's vast weight to throw
The line too labours, and the words move slow;
Not so, when swift Camilla scours the plain,
Flies o'er th'unbending corn, and skims along the main.

Expecting 10 and 11 year olds to be able to demonstrate control
of such a complex skill was a tall order, of course. I was satisfied
that they seemed to appreciate the effects Pope had achieved and
be conscious of contrasts of pace and sound quality. Most were
able to write something using 'contrasting sounds' at a fairly
simple level, by using long lines contrasted with short ones, and
words from a 'gentle words' list that they prepared, contrasted
with more violent vocabulary:

SOUNDING PICTURE – CONTRASTS

The lion moves slowly through the long grass
trying not to make a sound
it purrs softly, quietly moving closer to its prey
then with a great roar it lashes out its fierce paws
    and grabs the dear
    tearing
    ripping it apart

Karrie Blake (11)

or by setting up a regular rhythm and then shattering it with a capitalised yell,

> I'm glumb and I'm dumb and I'm bored
> I'm dumb and I'm glumb and I'm bored
> I'm bored and I'm glumb and I'm dumb
> I'm bored and I'm dumb and I'm glumb
> I've got loads of toys but I'm still bored
> Suddenly my mum called
> **SAMMY SAMMY**
> I called back
> **WHAT**
> And she said
>
> Your dad's got a day off so we can take you to the fair
> **YIPPEE I CAN'T WAIT**
> I started jumping around everywhere
> And I had a good day after all.

Samantha Parsons (10)

One pupil, however, made conscious use of Pope's technique for slowing a line down, the three-strong-beats cluster ('hoarse, rough verse', 'rock's vast weight', 'line too labours', and 'words move slow'):

THE SMASHED CAR

> The car zips along the road,
> Faster than a bullet from a gun,
> Zoom there it goes rushing,
> Whizzing through towns and villages,
> Then BOOM,
> Ford car dies,
> No more rush
> Everything silent,
>
> All you can hear is a crackle and a pop.

Gareth Mault (10)

'Ford car dies' and 'No more rush' are rhythmically very sophisticated poetic effects.

Four Steps to Song Construction

The first stage of the song-writing project itself, after these warm-up exercises on aural awareness, was to make word lists of like-sounding items. We did this initially as part of a 'sound contrasts' lesson. The 'feeling' connotations of words are, of course, to a large extent bound up in their *meanings*, but some of the words have been chosen purely for their sound, independent of the meaning, and this gives rise to irony – a fascinating tension between the various aspects of a word – as in Oliver's extraordinary choice of the word 'war':

GENTLE SOUNDING WORDS

soft
hockey
wine
war
peach
apple

Oliver Whiddett (10)

UGLY SOUNDING WORDS

strong	fungus	heave
broad	grease	break
grand	zit	broke
smack	bite	jaw
nut	bell	wack
thud	bang	punch
hurt		

Ryan Clements (11)

The second stage was to combine them into patterned groups of sound:

GENTLE WORDS

Tiny soft leaf
Sweet soft tissue
Smooth secret poem
Love sound music
Secret music sound
Secret music poem

Darran (11)

From this procedure we can already see some interesting

phrases emerging which creatively yoke words in combinations that would never arise from writing within a rational framework of meaning. We can leave all these on one side, to be called upon later for refrains, and offer a choice of two approaches to the song subjects to the class: they can either start writing descriptions of character based on a selection of pictures provided (for more detailed comments on the selection of pictures, see Chapter 8) or start writing short narratives to match the mood of their word clusters. The rough narratives will be shaped into evenly matched line lengths, but there is no great difficulty involved in telling a story in a few lines and pupils of all abilities can cope with the task. Accordingly, some members of the class start writing using the pictures; others simply take the 'mood' of their word lists as the starting point for a short narrative.

In the fourth stage, the picture-poem is seen as 'the verse'. Suitable phrases are chosen from the grouped word lists to be the refrain. Or the narrative lines are seen as short 'verses' to be edited together with a sound-word refrain. Splicing and editing are processes that force many word-aware decisions from the young. They make sophisticated choices, with some awareness of the professional lyricist's craft:

I AM AN ARTIST

(From a photograph of Matisse, when old, with a model, by Brassai, 1939)

I am an artist, [*triangle*]
Painting flowers and things [*cymbals*]
Sweet soft music, painting all the time [*all sing*]

I paint with great care [*tri*] and I stare [*cym*]
Breeze season leaf, painting all the time [*all*]

I am an old man [*tri*] painting a young woman [*cym*]
Hello love sound, painting all the time [*all*]

I wish I was younger [*tri*] so I could be with her [*cym*]
Tiny piece tissue, painting all the time [*all*]

Just like the old days [*tri*] with the younger ones [*cym*]
Smooth swift secret, painting all the time [*all, repeat*]

Ben Dootson (11)

THE STRICT MAN

(From a portrait of Herwarth Walden by Oskar Kokoschka)

The man comes home tired, restless, helpless
   Lashing storm crack bang
   Tough fist hard power
   Hack kill bull
He takes it out on his children, stick, belt
   Lashing storm crack bang
   Tough fist hard power
   Hack kill bull
The boy grabs the belt, father fights
   Lashing storm crack bang
   Tough fist hard power
   Hack kill bull
The man is dead tne boy runs
   Lashing storm crack bang
   Tough fist hard power
   Hack kill bull
The boy feels guilty, ashamed forever
   Lashing storm crack bang
   Tough fist hard power
   Hack kill bull

Scott Attrill and John Paul Barrett (11)

I think this is probably unfair on poor Herwarth Walden, who looks quite civilized to me, but it no doubt owes something to the storm of publicity about child abuse in 1987.

Ryan, author of the following, has a 'tin ear' which cannot hear rhythms or match lines without expending agonised labour counting and guessing, but he has succeeded in the task nonetheless. In the next activity, performance, he proved to be a star, confident with an audience and full of 'bazzaz'.

HEAVYWEIGHT

Mike Tyson steps in the ring
Thomas sweats to the bone
   Broad punch broke jaw
   Zit bang whack
Three rounds have gone of boxing hard
Thomas aches with pain
   Broad punch   *etc.*

This round Tyson knows he's won
This is the end – down he goes
Broad punch   *etc.*

Ryan (11)

The class that has reached this point will be able to pick up on ideas quickly and shape them with a sense of what they might become as songs or poems, but on the first attempt they find it difficult because they do not know, cannot know, where they are aiming. The teacher, accordingly, has to be rather more directive than he or she would like, steering pupils towards structured song forms by displaying a vision of the promised land, backed up by encouraging exhortations and sheepdog dashes to cut them off from unfruitful lines of development.

The song-writing projects emphasised two particular aspects of gaining conscious control over language: a high level of awareness of the contrasting sound qualities of words and experience of editing chunks of text from different sources to make a new text. The first is intended to develop general sensitivity to language. The second is, I hope, habit-forming. It certainly would be if reinforced. Pupils should in future understand that a report in science or history might be improved by cutting and pasting paragraphs in another order; that elements from two different pieces of writing can be combined effectively; that writing can be built up systematically step by step; and that you can not only rewrite a *sentence* and a *paragraph*, but also confidently mould the whole structure into a new unity.

If you do plan to write formally regular songs, like ballads, you will need to listen to recordings with the class and explicitly analyse the structural elements: hook lines (in pop songs); refrains; number of beats in a line; rhyme-scheme and stanza pattern. You are in danger of receiving a lot of derivative pop song lyrics full of clichéd sentiment if you just introduce the structure and ask for a song, though. Careful planning is needed to ensure that subjects are fresh and that thought goes into the *phrasing* before all attention is focused on tunes and on fitting the line and rhyme structure. Once pupils have charged ahead and are clamouring round you, 'Sir! We've finished our song! Can we sing it now?' it is a bit late to take them back to the beginning and gently hint that they could be less superficial in the treatment of the subject.

7 Haiku, Triolets, Villanelles and Pantoums

We are now going to look at some forms of verse that highlight elements of construction. The haiku serves to exemplify principles of conciseness, concreteness and word choice; the other forms considered introduce the aspects of line length, repetition, rhyming and the use of interwoven patterns for interwoven meanings.

I have not attempted in this chapter to give an exhaustive guide to forms; I have selected as examples a few which are successful at all ability levels. Haiku have been imperfectly understood and the troubadour forms are little known in schools. They offer great opportunities for learning to control language.

There are many other formal verse structures one can use in the classroom, from the simple structures of formula poems (add a rule about following a set number of syllables for rhythmic regularity) and the rhythmic patterns described in Chapter 6, to iambic blank verse and, with older pupils, ballads and even sonnets.

To introduce iambic rhythm, enjoy the game of iambic conversations. It takes a little practice and has to be emphatically articulated with alternating stresses but can soon be managed by most children:

'Hello, I see you've got your trainers on!

'Oh yes, I kick a ball around at break.' etc.

Do not imagine, however, that ballads are easy. Only a few children will succeed in mastering the form well enough to use it expressively. I have found that even adult BA literature students need a lot of help to control the stresses. Keeping the line lengths to a regular pattern while controlling the rhyme and the sense is tricky enough, but in addition the rhythm has a habit of slipping from duple time to triple time without the writer noticing:

Killer Michael Ryan loved his mum.

'I'll protect you and see that you're happy,' she said.

Haiku

The haiku is a Japanese poem with seventeen syllables, which is usually, but by no means always, translated as three lines of five, seven and five syllables. Many translators do not render the haiku in seventeen syllables at all. It is useful to aim at seventeen syllables with children, but sharp observation and an awareness of the relationship of the parts within a very small verbal construct are the important features. Sandy Brownjohn, Pie Corbett, Brian Moses and other commentators suggest that we conceive of it as a 'snapshot'. This word rightly suggests the pictorial, arrested, small-scale, observant and precise qualities of haiku. It is only half the story, however, and I should like to dwell for a moment on the other, neglected, half. What the 'snapshot' view leaves out is the Zen Buddhist reverence that goes into the observation, the quality of 'is-ness' or 'such-ness' that is evoked, the view of the world as 'just as it is' (which in Japanese is called *sono-mama*). As one of the pre-haiku 'Zenrin Kushu' couplets has it:

Taking up one blade of grass
Use it as a sixteen-foot golden Buddha.

A reverent sense of the life in the blade of grass, the 'insignificant' object observed, is essential to a really resonant haiku, though reverence does not mean solemnity. An old Zen story tells of a novice monk who spent years meditating to prepare a profound question for his master and asked, 'What is the Buddhahood?' The master, 'T'ung-shan, snapped at him, 'Three pounds of flax!' This robust, surreal answer is the extreme of the more conventional, haiku:

Buddha:
cherry flowers
in moonlight

Hoitsu (1760–1828) *trans*. Stryk and Ikemoto

In the following haiku, one observation is enough to give a vivid impression of the priorities of life in a peasant village, its mean competitive triumphs and the character of the farmer. The poem relishes the vitality of the 'trivial', but it is not solemn!

> Transplanting rice,
> he pisses
> in a crony's field.
>
> Yayu *trans*. Stryk and Ikemoto

The starting point for haiku classes is to learn something of the Japanese tradition and savour a few examples. *The Penguin Book of Zen Poetry* is a good source.

> You light the fire;
>   I'll show you something nice, –
>   A great ball of snow!
>
> Basho *trans*. R. H. Blyth

> Alas, under a helmet
> is crushed a grasshopper
>
> Basho *trans*. Hiroko Hiraishi

> The sparrow
> hops along the veranda
> with wet feet
>
> Shiki

> Are there
> short-cuts in the sky,
> summer moon?
>
> Lady Sute-Jo *trans*. Stryk and Ikemoto

Each of these has the quality of vividly evoking a much fuller scene than is described – a scene with a history, characters, smells, texture and a precise associated feeling. As is usual in traditional haiku, a clue to the season is given (e.g. in the second one above, the grasshopper suggests autumn).

It helps if pupils are told that Japanese poets spend a lifetime studying and perfecting the 'simple' seventeen syllable form; that the Japanese read a haiku twice through and then leave a silence; that the poems are objects of meditation inviting the reader to participate; and that the most admired ones hint at a whole landscape in a detail, express stillness in movement, mutability and permanance together, unity in diversity.

> Contending –
> temple bell,
> winter wind,

> Kito (1740–89) *trans.* Stryk and Ikemoto

Obviously, we are not teaching Zen Buddhist meditation, but a whole dimension is missing from the haiku if you do not catch something of the sense of wonder and surprise of finding that a dull-looking tight bud of a poem has unfolded into a world of colour and fragrance.

Although I am making grand claims for the profundity of great haiku, you should never set large themes (like 'Eternity and Time', 'Age', 'Joy' or 'Love') as subjects. A quality of something like 'loneliness', or a sense of the solitary and quiet (known as *sabi*) is one of the four characteristic 'moods' of Japanese haiku, but it is the aftertaste of the poem, not its ostensible subject.

> With the evening breeze,
> The water laps against
> The heron's legs.

> *trans.* R. H. Blyth

Haiku-writing is an excellent discipline for learning many of the principles of good writing. Pupils learn to write from observation, not abstraction. They see the implications of a visual image that is clear and concrete and recognise the force of the advice, 'Show, don't tell'. They have to conserve words and weigh their value: all superfluous verbiage is cut. They learn that the form has a history and prestige, and is to be honoured.

Garry, a streetwise inner-city 11 year old, not noted for a reverential disposition, wrote:

> The grass is ever green
> It's never young never old
> It seems to live on

> Garry Wiltshire

He came to this by lying face down on the school field looking at grass, not by being invited to philosophise about life and death. All you are likely to get if you aim for profundity is portentousness; but if you aim for a sharp eye picking out something worth attending to you might get poetry.

> Garry messing about
> Showing off in front of friends
> Giggling, laughing, rest.

> Jason Mullineaux (11)

In the above piece about Garry (the same Garry), the last word has to do a lot of work, modest and still though it is, but Jason knows that haiku are read with care, twice, and that you visualise them and savour them, so he is confident that his last syllable can cope with the weight of the other sixteen. It works well because the action is already past its climax and there is a running down of energy in 'Giggling, laughing. . .' and an expectation of finality and stillness at the end of a poem anyway. Tony (12) also lay looking at the grass and came up with a suggestively universal image:

> BLADE

> The blade of grass
> sits waving in the wind
> with millions surrounding it

> Tony Mayo

Tony's piece started life as:

> The bright green blade of grass
> sits alone
> waving in the wind –

His second draft has dispensed with the superfluous adjectives ('bright', 'green'), dropped the vaguely sentimental 'alone' in favour of the infinitely more suggestive image of isolation within abundant company – this may have been a response to thinking about my challenge, 'What do you mean by *alone*? There's plenty of grass!' – and is a completed thought rather than an unfinished fragment. Haiku can teach this kind of sensitivity to the effects of words and the satisfying shape of a completed thought. Watch Lee, a girl of 10, thinking:

Draft 1

> A leaf floats in through the classroom / window

~~like a feather~~ and lands ~~alone~~
crumpled
like a crisp packet (*later addition*)

Draft 2

FLOATING

A leaf floats in through the classroom window
and lands crumpled
like a crisp
    packet

Lee Baldwin

Draft 1

A lead on my pencil writing what I write. Obeying my command.
like a slave who has no choice.

She rejects this in favour of:

Draft 2

A lead on my pencil writing what I write
like a shadow
    trailing behind me

Lee Baldwin

Just one more example, of many possible ones: Jason, 11, develops the potential of his word 'washing' through successive drafts until he has a clear and completed thought. He does not need my help; he just needs to be in an environment where writing is taken seriously and his craftsmanship will be appreciated. There is a willow in the school field – the following is based on an observation.

Draft 1

WEEPING LIKE A WILLOW

The big willow waved
washing away the cold breeze
~~Then laying to rest~~

added: ~~Leaving a fresh bark~~
added: leaving fresh branches.

Draft 2   The big willow waved
Washing away the breeze

Leaving fresh branches

Jason Mullineaux

I should add here that deleting the intended title is an improvement. Sandy Brownjohn recommends titling haiku to afford extra syllables and to teach the value of a title that adds something, but I think untitled haiku have more freedom to do their work.

Haiku are not always well taught and William J. Higginson and Ron Padgett are right to complain, in *The Whole World Catalogue 2*, about 'the pious and sentimental generalities so often poured into the 5–7–5 syllable form' (Higginson) and the 'sugar' (Padgett). Higginson abandons the syllabic structure and works on 'images', and Padgett instructs his pupils to make the third line 'something that has nothing to do with the first two lines', in the hope of getting surprising juxtapositions of images. The results are not impressive, though he seems pleased. Corbett and Moses, in *Catapults and Kingfishers*, subdivide the haiku into a first line on the 'time of day', a second which is to 'focus on something' and a third in which you 'compare it to something else'. This produces better results but the verse can become predictable and may not have the scope of 'proper' haiku. The solution to the problem of superficial, sentimental haiku is to teach pupils to discriminate between easy sentimentality and real perception, to avoid abstractions and to keep the original observation in focus; it is not to change the form into something else.

Younger age-groups can grasp the idea very successfully:

Trees waving in the wind
rain thunders down
trees loosen their roots

Cheese on toast
Lovely and warm
Mum is hard at work

(Class Mac, Emsworth First School, 7 year olds)

And here are two more examples from middle school children:

Wayne runs down the wing
With deep thoughts of Wembley
Crash – he's tackled again

David Amies (11)

The sun is angry
and burning my skin
what have I done to him?

Ami-Louise Reid (10)

I wrote some as well, to show willing. Here is one:

Our pampas-grass vandalised.
Somewhere there must be
a snug lined nest.

As Alan Watts writes, in *The Way of Zen*, 'The artificial *haiku* always feels like a piece of life which has been deliberately broken off or wrenched away from the universe, whereas the genuine *haiku* has dropped off all by itself, and has the whole universe inside it'.

I find the haiku a very successful form with children. Of the other five-line to eight-line forms, the cinquain and triolet are also well adapted to classroom use. (Much more so than the tanka which, although often recommended in the same breath as the haiku, lacks its conciseness and is much more difficult for a Westerner to master.) The cinquain is relatively well known, but the triolet is seldom described and so I shall devote the next section to its balanced, circular strength.

Triolets

The triolet is a mediaeval French troubadour form, like the villanelle and pantoum discussed later, and the ballade, rondel, rondelet, rondeau, chant royal, lai, kyrielle and sestina. All these forms have elaborately patterned stanza structures with complex rhyme schemes, and most are far too rigid for comfort and fiendishly over-ingenious. The attractive feature of the forms is the notion of repeating certain lines in a set pattern – a subtler and more varied effect of refrain. The simplest of the forms is the rondel as used here by François Villon, not the more highly-wrought later development of the rondel:

Jenin L'Avenu,
Va-t-en aux estuves,
Et toy là venu,
Jenin l'Avenu,
Si te lave nud

Et te baigne és cuves,
Jenin l'Avenu.

An English version of this which retains the rhyme scheme and its informal charm is by Mervyn Savill:

Little John of the Square
To the baths then, you cub!
And when you get there,
Little John of the Square.
Strip yourself bare
And bathe in the tub,
Little John of the Square.

The triolet form repeats the first line in the middle and at the end too, but is a little longer (eight lines) and gets an even more emphatic sense of circularity because the second line is repeated at the end as well as the first. Like the rondel it has only two rhymes. The simplified form of triolet I adapted for use with children has only one rhyme, apart from the inevitable rhymes of repetition, to round off the ending on a chime:

THE TRIOLET PATTERN
Pattern of lines and rhyme

1	line one
2	line two
3	new line
4	line one [*repeated*]
5	new line
6	new line [*must rhyme with line two*]
7	line one repeated
8	line two repeated

SCARRED
(Story from the *Daily Mirror*)

1	She scarred me for life
2	Says her toy boy lover
3	I opened the door
4	She scarred me for life
5	She threw a boiling kettle
6	And now I will suffer
7	She scarred me for life
8	Says her toy boy lover.

Emma and Sarah (11)

I introduced the class to triolets with one from Wendy Cope beginning, 'I used to think all poets were Byronic' (Cope, 1986), and an unwieldy Gavin Ewart with its own revolting appeal, all about a disgusting menu, called 'A McGonagall-type Triolet on *the Full revoltingness of Commercial Fast Food*' (Ewart, 1985) but both of these were brittle, coy, ironic adult verses, not really suitable models for the pupils to follow. I therefore composed a couple of my own to set the tone. It seemed to me that the repetition had an insistent quality of warning, and would lend itself well to subjects that were sinister and hinted at mystery. The first started:

TRIOLET – SHE RETURNS FROM ABROAD

The eyes did not smile
They stared green fire. . .

The second was:

TRIOLET – WHAT HURT YOU SO?

Why do you cry mother?
What hurt you so?
You pace the night garden
Why do you cry mother?
Why do you rip out
Our herbs where they grow?
Why do you cry mother?
What hurt you so?

They're not great but they served as a basis for me to discuss with the class my conception of the special opportunities offered by the triolet and provided an opportunity to examine the structure. The first one maintained the strict rhyme scheme of its first two lines but in the second I used my simplified system where just line six rhymes with the last line (also line two). It may also have helped that I became a writer like my pupils and talked about the problems I had had, disclosing my own hesitations and doubts about word choice. It is not important that you are a *good* writer, only that you *are* a writer.

The subjects I proposed for them to try the form were: lines from a newspaper story; 'something scary' – signs of unhappiness, of a secret, of an animal's odd behaviour or of something wrong; or lines about a character, taken from a previous piece of their writing. In the event they almost all chose to write 'something scary.

WHAT WAS IT?

She sat by the fire
Her face was dull and blank
Her eyes stared round the room
She sat by the fire
Why was she feeling sad?
What was it she had drank?
She sat by the fire
Her face was dull and blank.

Sarah Madden and Clare Jeffries (11)

One boy, who has a taste for 'Hammer Gothick', wrote a poem which was perhaps partly suggested by my lines about eyes that stared green fire but it was not a triolet:

THE DEVIL

She came home on a full moon
She didn't sound the same at all
When she talked her voice was deep
Her eyes glowed a brilliant red colour
She locks herself in a room
You hear noise – crash – then peace and quiet
I bashed the door down and stared
She was on the floor there dead
She'd slit her throat with a knife
She had a picture of the Devil
There alongside her on the floor.

John Paul Barrett (10)

I told him I loved the mysteriousness of the opening five lines in particular. I asked him to select lines from his poem and arrange them as a triolet. He was polite enough to humour me, and produced this arrangement:

TRIOLET: THE DEVIL

1   She came home on a full moon
2   When she talked her voice was deep
3   Her eyes glowed a brilliant red
4   She came home on a full moon
5   She locked herself in her room
6   You hear noise – crash – then sleep

7   She came home on a full moon
8   When she talked her voice was deep.

John Paul Barrett

John Paul still prefers his first gory version. I prefer the triolet and others in the class were divided about which was best, but the issue provoked a good critical discussion in which they were all involved as makers of verse, some appreciating understatement, mystery and the emphasis produced by the repetition of sinister lines, and others preferring all the gory details.

Two other boys wrote a poem that used the triolet pattern but needed a bit more space. They added four extra lines in the second half, but this did not destroy the echo:

1   It's not my fault dad lost his job
2   Being drunk on the job, starting fights
3   I'm in my bedroom playing with my toys
4   It's not my fault dad lost his job
5   Dad is sitting in the backroom reading
6   I hear him mumbling to himself
7   He calls my name, I do not answer
8   I hear him climbing the flight of stairs
9   Thump thump thump thump
10   I hear him switching on the lights
11   It's not my fault dad lost his job
12   Being drunk on the job, starting fights.

Danny Connolly (11) and Oliver Whiddett (10)

I should add that each of the last two poems quoted has been revised slightly by the boys concerned in the process of drafting final versions to even the line lengths and rhythms.

Villanelles

The 10 year old children took to triolets but found villanelles bafflingly perverse at first. A villanelle is, strictly speaking, a nineteen-line poem with only two rhymes, in five three-line stanzas (tercets) with a quatrain for the sixth and last stanza. The intriguing feature which makes it so suitable for creating a mood is the obsessive repetition of lines. The first and third lines crop up as the last lines of all the other tercets (line one in stanzas two and four, and line three in stanzas three and five) and again as the last two lines of the poem in the concluding quatrain. (See Robin Skelton's *The Practice of Poetry*, pp. 165–72 for a fuller historical discussion of examples of the villanelle.)

For our purposes, however, the villanelle in this form is too demanding. What I am presenting here as 'villanelles' are really poems of three or four lines, presented in varied permutations of repetition. Perhaps we should devise a glamorous new name for them – 'permunelles' or 'repeaters'?

Unfortunately, there are few accessible examples of villanelles to use as a means of introduction to younger age-groups. The one which delights them with its naughtiness, however, is Wendy Cope's 'Reading Scheme', in *Making Cocoa for Kingsley Amis*. With older age-groups, W. H. Auden's 'If I Could Tell You' and Ernest Dowson's chauvinist 'Villanelle of the Poet's Road' are suitable, and there is also a repeater, by John Mole called 'Song of the Diplomat', printed in the Brownjohns' *Meet and Write* Volume 2, with a prose explanation by John Mole.

Each repetition of a villanelle line has to be a self-contained statement that makes sense in any position in the poem, like a good refrain. The form seems suitable for subjects with inbuilt cycles of repetition and therefore I started with the expression of contradictory feelings, those ambivalent and paradoxical complexes of attraction and repulsion that go round and round in most of us.

Once again, I could not find a good example of a simplified verse without rhyme at the right comprehension level for the younger pupils so I wrote one myself which illustrated the point about alternations of feeling. It is an attempt to make four statements revolve around each other, representing the fluctuations in a relationship in a way I thought 11 year olds would understand. It is not particularly good poetry but it served its purpose in setting the scene for the villanelle writing task, a game demanding ingenuity.

VILLANELLE – FOR MY SON

I love your cheerful funny way of being
You're open, keen to learn, alert and fond
But when you close me out it drives me mad

In the end we talk and listen well
You're open, keen to learn, alert and fond
But when you close me out it drives me mad

When you drive me mad I close you out
Though in the end we talk and listen well
You're open, keen to learn, alert and fond
I love your cheerful funny way of being.

This was the model on which two boys constructed a pattern based on four statements about their girlfriends, though they didn't follow quite the same sequence of repetitions:

MY BIRD SANDRA / MY BIRD KERRY

I like your personality, I like your lovely hair
When you talk to other boys my feelings are really bad
When I'm in a cop you smile and I calm down

I will always comfort you and always keep you warm
When you talk to other boys my feelings are really bad
I like your personality, I like your lovely hair

I will always comfort you and always keep you warm
When I'm in a cop you smile and I calm down
I like your personality, I like your lovely hair

Ben Dootson (Sandra) Ryan Clements (Kerry) (11)

Realising that most pupils would need some secure basis for the writing of villanelles, I prepared extracts from newspaper stories for them to manipulate into patterns of repeating lines. This proved difficult and I conceived a new respect for Emma and Sarah, whose triolet based on a *Daily Mirror* story is quoted above. They had taken a headline which happened to have an appropriate rhythm – *She Scarred Me For Life Says Her Toy Boy Lover* – and used it for their poem. When I came to select story lines with the same rhythmic strength I found that most journalistic writing needs adapting to fit into line units. I provided my own adapted selection of what I thought were appropriately matched lines, along with the original newspaper stories to groups in the class and they worked from them. I am glad to say they also made their own adaptations to suit their purposes and devised ways of solving their formal problems:

I WANT MY NOSE BACK!

(Villanelle based on story in *The Sun*, 1 July 1987)

A mad vampire thug was hunted last night
Bob's mother Irene said, 'It was a nightmare'

'I hope the person who bit Bob is proud of what he's done!'

He plunged his teeth into Bob's neck then bit off his nose
Bob's mother Irene said, 'It was a nightmare'
'I hope the person who bit Bob is proud of what he's done!'

He plunged his teeth into Bob's neck then bit off his nose
Bob's mother Irene said, 'It was a nightmare'
A mad vampire thug was hunted last night

Carol O'Shea, Rachel Colverson, and Emily (10 and 11)

The line above about 'proud of what he's done' is overlong but
it was too funny to omit. Another group chose to use a selection
of headlines from one day's *Daily Mirror*, but their interpretation
of the repeating-lines task is a long way from being a villanelle –
it really amounts to using one line as a refrain every three lines.
However, they achieved a sense of rhythm and used rhyme quite
successfully and, as I learned from trying it myself, it is a tricky
skill to manipulate 'journalese' into a coherent pattern:

HEADLINES

The headlines in the paper
Arsenal boss is full of greed
Interest credit now is free

The headlines in the paper
Have a problem? Write to Marje
If, my dear, you are very large

The headlines in the paper
Boy dies of Superglue
A streetwise tart in tears is new

The headlines in the paper
17,000 pounds a week
For Banking boss, that's very neat
The headlines in the paper

Sarah Madden and Clare Jeffries (11)

I tried the villanelle form with a couple of 15 year olds to see
if they took to them without the hesitations of the 10 year
olds. Barnaby successfully used the villanelle's repetitiveness to
represent a 'monotonous chain' (as he said) of enslavement to
work; in another poem, he used it to represent the predictability

of television 'repeats'; and then he developed his own version of
the villanelle, a three-line pattern of repetition in changing
sequence, using short lines for comic effect;

WINDOW CLEANING

Dip the chamois in the bucket
Up the ladder, down the ladder
Wiping dirty windows

Down the ladder, up the ladder
Wiping dirty windows
In the bucket dip the chamois

Wiping dirty windows
Dip the chamois in the bucket
Up the ladder, down the ladder.

Barnaby Jafkins (15)

For all these subjects the boring circularity of repetition was
highly appropriate. Jesse, also 15, took another cyclical subject,
perhaps suggested by the W. H. Auden villanelle. He had to
revise his draft to get odd line lengths to match and his fourth
line went through various rewrites, from the bureaucratic 'An old
man terminates his existence', to the simpler but undistinguished
'slowly dies', to a line that takes its cue from the 'morning' of
line two.

LIFE CIRCLE – A VILLANELLE

Life goes round as you will see
A cheeky baby is born in the morning
We trudge through life 'til we're exhausted
A knowing old man watches the sunset

We trudge through life 'til we're exhausted
A knowing old man watches the sunset
A cheeky baby is born in the morning

Life goes round as you will see
A knowing old man watches the sunset
A cheeky baby is born in the morning
We trudge through life 'til we're exhausted

Jesse (15)

Pantoums

Lastly, I shall give examples of another of these obsessive troubadour forms, the pantoum. The pantoum has an appealing chain structure in which lines two and four of each quatrain become lines one and three of the following one. For my purposes, I decided to limit the form to three stanzas and bring the unrepeated lines from stanza one into the last stanza to round it off. I gave out the following guide to the class with a couple of warning notes appended:

THE PANTOUM PATTERN

Line pattern	No.	Rhyme	Write lines here
line 1	1	a	
line 2	2	b	
line 3	3	a	
line 4	4	b	
line 2 repeat	5	b	
new line	6	c	
line 4 repeat	7	b	
new line	8	c	
line 6 repeat	9	c	
line 1 repeat	10	a	
line 8 repeat	11	c	
line 3 repeat	12	a	

Notes

Each line will have to make sense on its own!
Each line will have to be able to fit in at the beginning, middle or end of the story.

This was the only form of the pantoum attempted with the 10 year olds (at this stage the children were choosing from newspaper stories and triolets as well and many were busy rehearsing songs) but it was successful enough to suggest that the form might be a fertile one for children:

PANTOUM

Light is the day
Dark is the night
Sweet is the sugar
Bitter the salt

Dark is the night
Good is the child
Bitter is the salt
Bad is the man

Good is the child
Light is the day
Bad is the man
Sweet is the sugar

Lianne (11)

My 15 year old guinea pigs found a good subject for the form in pleas:

IT'S SUICIDE

Standing on the edge
'Don't do it!'
Don't jump off the ledge
It's not worth it.

'Don't do it!'
Don't be a fool.
It's not worth it
Just keep your cool.

Don't be a fool
Standing on the edge
Just keep your cool.
Don't jump off the ledge.

Barnaby Jafkins (15)

These troubadour forms provide a good introduction to some of the techniques of crafting words into patterns. Pupils manipulate phrases to fit the formal constraints, which forces them to look beyond their first idea and seek an alternative word order, or to say the same thing more succinctly. The triolet demands one rhyme. That is not too much to cope with, unlike the confusing rhymes of ballad-like stanzas – the rhyming tail ends up wagging the dog and the sense is lost. The one rhyme binds the ending into the poem and pupils learn to prepare for the strong effect of a chiming last line. The pantoum demands greater skill in rhyming and is too complicated for less confident pupils.

All the troubadour forms have a solid quality – they will not fall over or blow away – and serve to show how form can give substance to impressions and how repetition is a powerful rhetorical device. In some cases, the cyclical form becomes a significant part of the meaning and conveys the message that 'life goes round in circles; what goes up must come down; this routine is monotonous and repetitive; or, everything relates to everything else in a neverending sequence of opposition and reconciliation'. If using the forms makes some pupils aware of how the choice of an appropriate form in itself can solve problems of expression, then an important aspect of critical understanding has been absorbed. The point that all will be able to internalise, however, is that one can shape the building-blocks of meaning, the lines, and 'cut' and 'paste' them in an editorial process to gain rhetorical effects. With reinforcement, this knowledge will be retained and can be used on all writing tasks. The teacher should make a point of inviting pupils to discuss their experiences and note their thoughts in the journal (see Chapter 10) in order to bring to full consciousness their sense of the skills they have used – so that they know that they know what they know. Some will express a sense of relief and release when they discover that writing is not a runaway train, as they had feared.

8 Texts – Pictures and Portraits

A NONSENSE POEM

He knows that I like him
    and
I know he likes me
    but
He wont say anything
    as
They all know that I like him
    and
He likes me
    and therefore
He wont say anything to me.

I know that they know
    so
I wont say anything
    either.
He knows that they know
    and
He wont say anything
    so
We both know really
    but
Wont say anything.

Wendy Poppleton (14)

Wendy's poem arose out of reading R. D. Laing's *Knots* and seeing how his way of expressing his insights into human behaviour can illuminate her sense of the absurdity of a relationship she feels she has with a boy in the class (which has remained unacknowledged and silent). The use of plaintive conjunctions between lines is Wendy's own formal device but perfectly

appropriate to the halting logic of the subject. Laing's poems
have 'inspired' Wendy. This means that she has been stimulated
by his intelligence, borrowed his technique of constructing a
circular argument out of simple emotional statements, and used
his example to *further her own thought*. She could never have
developed the whole vision of a psychology implicit in this poem
from her own introspection, but she readily apprehends it in
Knots and is able to leap into Laing's level of understanding and
use it to express her own feelings.

Texts 'inspire' us: they provide a framework for our perceptions
and a focus for our enquiry; our thoughts are shaped by the fine
hearts and minds of writers and artists who have gone before;
imagination and intelligence are nourished on 'culture . . . the
best that has been known and said in the world, and thus . . .
the history of the human spirit,' as Matthew Arnold grandly put
it.

There is an infinite number of texts. (I shall use this term,
following current practice, to refer to songs, pictures, TV
programmes, poems, objects or anything else that is used for
pupils to 'read'.) Literary texts make marvellous models for
writing (see Kenneth Koch's *Rose, Where Did You Get That Red?*
for unusual examples of children's writing based on famous
poems); some teachers use music successfully, though it is too
abstract for me; but I have chosen in this chapter to use
visual texts as examples. The principles I discuss – questioning
technique and the criteria for selection – apply equally to all
other kinds of texts used as stimuli or triggers for writing.

How To Talk About Texts

Discussion of a text for a creative purpose is not the same as
critical discussion, but in both cases the quality of the questions
you pose is crucial to the success of the lesson. Questions should
lead the pupils more deeply into the rich world of the subject
and help them to experience its special qualities. About a
landscape painting, for example, the question, 'Where do you
think this place might be?' will not lead anywhere except to
fruitless guessing, but, 'What adventures would you have in this
place?' leads into an exploration of the picture and an imaginative
involvement in the place it depicts. 'What animals do you think
might live here?' might be an appropriate critical question in a

science lesson but is not going to be useful for focusing the mind on the text itself.

The potential significance of a picture of, say, three human figures would be opened up by questions which explored relationships and character, like, 'What does the figure on the left feel about the one on the right?' or 'What is the central figure thinking?' or, 'Which of these people could you trust?' On the other hand, the subject would not be illuminated by questions like, 'Who are these people?' (inviting guesswork and fabrication masquerading as deducing conclusions from limited evidence) or, 'Tell the life history of the older figure' (which leads away from the subject into speculative and tiresome invention), or, 'Write about other people these figures remind you of' (why use a good painting or photograph if you do not ground your writing in its precise vision and vivid detail?) or, 'Why do these people wear hats?'. (I have heard a teacher use this one! He wanted to explain about heat loss through the head.)

The quality of texts

There are two principles to bear in mind when choosing a 'text'. It should be *of good quality* and it should be *open*.

Good quality means simply that the material offers sufficient interest and complexity for its potential range not to be quickly exhausted. You will not receive reflections on human character, full of sensitive insight, if your original text is a Mr Men cartoon. It is a mistake to believe that because such illustrations are supposedly part of the pupils' own 'culture' they will provide more effective resource material than a Goya, Daumier or Cruikshank cartoon. They are superficial; their purpose is to simplify human character, not to represent it as it is.

Nor will you get anything but a dribble of reflex sentimentality if you offer a chocolate-box picture of a kitten emerging from an old boot, or one of those glossy religious posters, very common in schools now, representing Nature's beauty at twilight and accompanied by an awe-struck quotation. Such texts are *not open*. They have designs on you. They want a particular response – 'Aaah!' in the one case and 'Isn't it lovely!' in the other – and the mind is neither stretched nor stimulated.

The notion of 'openness' applies to all kinds of 'text'. If the teacher has any secondary purpose – ideological, moral, religious, or curricular – which is additional to the writing purpose, then the activity is undermined and thought is closed down. The only loyalty that counts in a poetry-writing lesson is to the integrity of expression in language. What we are striving for is fidelity to experience and honesty. What we must avoid are received ideas and conventional sentiment. We teach pupils *how* to articulate, not *what* to articulate. That is a sufficient ideal. The proper place for moral and political debate is in the critical part of the writing programme. This occurs after the writing, when a writer's words are subject to scrutiny. There is a great difference between examining completed poems for authenticity and soundness, and signalling in advance what the 'right' moral conclusion should be.

To return to the visual, most great art can be relied upon not to foreclose on the response, so paintings tend to make good texts while photographs have to be selected with care.

For obvious reasons, advertising images have designs on you. You might think you can choose a suitable photograph from an advertisement, cut out the name of the product and be left with a good picture, but unfortunately it is not always the case. The photograph will still be presented in a visual style that determines the way you read its signs. Advertising images often contain complex embedded narratives and Freudian symbolism – excellent texts for *critical* exploration but never *open*, never suitable for creative development.

This is also true of glamorised images, from travel posters of Lake Geneva to photographs of film stars and pop stars in magazines. Cecil Beaton, Richard Avedon, and many great photographers have produced portraits of stars with interesting, lived-in faces, but it is a curious fact that actors, even wonderful old actors off duty, never look real in these portraits: they are always posing. Politicians, business people, passers-by, artists, in fact any kind of people except 'show biz' stars, make good subjects. This can create a difficulty for the teacher when selecting photographs from magazines. Family snaps and your own amateur photographs can provide good texts, if they have caught a character momentarily revealed, or the spirit of a place. Otherwise, you may have to turn to specialist collections. Non-glamorised photo-journalism is sometimes published in the Sunday colour supplements, but you need a surprising quantity of supplements to find enough good pictures for a class, so photography journals are better. Projected slides are the best texts for class discussion because everyone can see them at the same time, but for individual work do not neglect the humble postcard. Most art galleries sell postcards and a wide range of quality photographic art as well as painting and sculpture is now available on postcards.

Poets have often written about paintings. Sometimes they explore the subject of the picture, as in Shelley's 'On The Medusa of Leonardo da Vinci', Yeats' 'Lapis Lazuli', Auden's 'Musée des Beaux Arts', Philip Larkin's 'The Card Players' or William Carlos Williams' 'Pictures from Brueghel', and sometimes they pursue the nature of art, as in Keats' 'Ode on a Grecian Urn', or Browning's 'Fra Lippo Lippi' and 'Andrea del Sarto' monologues. Philip Larkin, in 'Lines on a Young Lady's Photograph Album' has apostrophized photography in lines of mock 'Muse-ment':

> But o, photography! as no art is,
> Faithful and disappointing! that records
> Dull days as dull, and hold-it smiles as frauds . . .

Recently a number of poets were commissioned to write about paintings in the Tate Gallery. One would expect a patchy collection of occasional verse but the poems are remarkably good – the writers have found rich and deep subjects to be images for their own preoccupations and meditations. Paintings, like poems, are machines to think with. They are interpretation-generators. The better the work of art, the more 'open' to interpretation it is, the more scope there is for observers to project themselves onto its canvas and see their own values in its new light. Propaganda has only one possible interpretation but a Van Gogh self-portrait is a text on which we can each recreate ourselves. Works of art help each other. Perhaps that is what Osip Mandelstam had in mind when he said, 'Poetry is like going up in a plane that manufactures and launches in mid-air another plane which flies off and makes and launches another one . . .'.

The poem below is a very fine example of a poem about a painting. It was a prizewinning entry in the W. H. Smith children's literary competition and published in the *Children As Writers* series.

7 AM BY EDWARD HOPPER

For Christmas they gave me a print
From a painting by Hopper.

He said all he wanted to do was 'paint
Sunlight on the side of a house'. So here
Painted sunlight falls on the ticking
Of a clock which shows the window the time, inaudibly.
The window shows an empty street a two-way gaze,
equivocal;
The columns stand indifferent,
Stretching the ground away from the roof.
This shop was made by people who were anxious
To demonstrate something,
Sneaked over the wood's boundary,
Built just beyond their rights,
Crowded the trees with an elbow
Of roads ground firm.

But the wood prospers,
In its unseen heart nurtures
Such a luscious green and a clamour
For soft, painted sunlight.
The wood has always been
Where it can do best, and
Angled clapboard, unfortunately,
Has no use for sun at present.
There appears to be no means of telling how far
The dew-wet wood spreads,
The silent path leads.
Why do the shelves stand empty?
The price is jammed in the till.
Do you see the unbearable blue of the sky's corner,
Or what isn't there, or is just beyond,
Is just behind, or inside?
What's left out must be better.

                                        Tabitha Tuckett (14)

The writer has meditated upon the relationships of sunlight and
clock; ground, column and roof; the man-made structure and
the 'unseen heart' of the wood; the empty shelves and jammed
till of a shop and the unknowable. In the course of this she has
somehow defined her own sense of excitement at what life beyond
the 'roads ground firm' might be like; she has also coined
memorable phrases and used stunning rhythmical effects – the
long sceptical, speculative line in a relaxed musing rhythm
followed by the short four soggy stresses of 'dew-wet wood
spreads' is perfect. (Where had she heard sounds like that? She
must have been a reader with a fine ear for rhythms.) The last

line, with a hint of Eve-like teenage relish and frustration, lightly puts a finger on a great paradox. Hopper's painting, the artistic text, has been the occasion for her beautifully intelligent movement towards articulating almost indefinable aspects of her sense of life; it has been the framework for her thinking and feeling her way to the clarity of language.

Needless to say, the quality of Hopper's vision is an element in the poem and a chain-store print of horses in the surf would not have served in the same way. Sentimental 'art', like those prancing stallion images, adds up to a *closed* sign meaning 'freedom, and virile muscularity!' which puts a stop to your thinking, whereas the *openness* of Hopper's painting is most eloquently attested by the growing urgency and excitement of Tabitha Tuckett's ever-sharper series of questions.

Pictures

In the rest of the chapter I shall give examples of writing which involved pupils in responding to pictorial texts. I shall also discuss examples which came about as a result of an integrated project on portraiture. The writing furnishes further examples of the two kinds of drafting: the sensitive editing of first attempts and the building up of a piece of writing through planned sequences.

Pictures can lead average pupils to a precise use of language and a sustained form of observant attention. Writing is more articulate by the middle years of schooling than conversational speech. In writing one loses gesture, intonation, facial expression and the conspiratorial 'Y'know!' and makes up for them with more considered statements of greater precision. At least one does if the writing is not a matter of copying (called *'research'*) or answering questions using the words already provided. A good quality open text welcomes this precision and has a great deal to reveal to the keen eye.

THE OLD MAN

(From a photograph of Jean Renoir in 1972 by Richard Avedon)

> His lips aren't the tight sort, they are rather loose
> He looks as if his face has been moulded out of plasticene
> He looks like an old bloodhound
> He looks as though he's got no one to care for him

His head is the shape of a boiled egg
Look into his eyes and you will see sadness

Carol O'Shea (11)

Not a great deal of redrafting has gone into this, but the lines
were numbered and reordered, and one line was dropped ('This
is the old man we feel sorry for', on the writing principle 'Show
don't tell'). It is not highly sensitive to words but it represents
work on the right lines by any normal pupil, looking a bit beyond
the first impressions and trying to be more precise in description.
It is writing-as-a-way-of-developing-articulacy rather than poetry-
as-art, the daily stuff of writing classes with all pupils.

The next example is similar but has a more developed stanza
pattern.

SHE IS

(From the portrait of Elizabeth Brandt by Peter Paul Rubens)

Warm, motherly, smug
but sweet

She reminds me of a daisy
she reminds me of a daisy
warm and kind

Humorous, sharp, kind
but witty

Chorus

Caring, truthful, comical
and quick

Chorus

crafty, brainy, friendly
and beautiful

Sophie and Rachel (11)

Sophie and Rachel successfully grouped their impressions into
stanzas of contrasting qualities, suggesting the interesting complexity of the personality of the sitter, but had most trouble with
their chorus. They rejected their first ideas, 'As clever as a dog'
and 'Sharp as a needle', as not sufficiently warm for their
purposes, but have chosen to make do with the hackneyed
comparison 'daisy', which comes loaded with connotations of
simple childlike innocence as well as the connotations they
sought.

I have mostly quoted character sketches based on portraits here, but landscapes, cityscapes and seascapes all offer the imagination scope to roam, and pictures that appear to be part of a story invite identification with a character's situation and can also provide a framework for expressing one's own doubts and fears.

ESCAPE

(From 'Dame nature gives her orders to Genius', an illuminated page from a Harley manuscript, *Roman de la Rose*, British Museum postcard)

> The princess is planning to escape.
> Imagine the thoughts on her mind
> The pressures
> Who can she rely on?
> Who can she trust?
>
> No one.

Mark (11)

The following marvellous poem enters into the spirit of the picture, a portrait, by holding a dialogue with the sitter. It owes a lot, no doubt, to the support of the classteacher who seems to have encouraged pupils to give voice to their humour, morbidity and sensitivity – to the full range of their personalities.

ADMIRAL SIR RICHARD VESEY HAMILTON

I see you in two ways,
At first glance I thought you were an old
Kindly man,
But I began to see through your disguise.
I imagine you're the sort of person
Who tricks people into the slaughter-house.
Once they were in you would turn nasty,
Bite their heads off!
You're a proud man,
But somewhere in you there is still a small
Kind person.
I imagine that you are built to command
Ships and men,
If you weren't so tidy you would probably carry a whip,
I suppose someone else carries it for you,
Do they?

William Passingham (11)

People and Portraits

Good quality texts for the observant description of people are also provided in the form of British soap operas, which pupils follow avidly (they are by far the most popular programmes). Some characters are two-dimensional stock characters, but many of them are rounded human portraits. They possess fine qualities as well as weaknesses, they have history and grow into personalities that the pupils come to know intimately. They have the enormous advantage to teachers of being known to all the class and so, unlike a person known only to one or two pupils, they can be discussed in detail, and understandings and judgements can be shared. This, of course, is the function of a common culture.

ANGIE WATTS' THOUGHTS

I felt happy that Den was showing more interest in me,
not knowing that he came home because he had an
argument with his bit of stuff.
Den, I wouldn't wonder, would probably be with her now.
I don't really hate Jan,
but then again I don't really like her.
I feel sorry for him because I love him.
I don't think it's really worth it,
running after him all the time.
I love him, and he loves her.

                                        Rachael Lilley (10) in 1986

There is yards and yards of this stuff in some pupils (the above is extracted from a longer piece with comments on many other characters and a narrative of recent events). With 9 and 10 year olds, most of it is retelling, without much analysis, evaluation or penetration of motives, though it may be well organised as narrative, and genuinely empathetic, and may be accurately imaginative in the way it enters into another's voice ('bit of stuff' is an authentic Angie phrase). The evaluation and analysis of motives can be developed by the teacher through discussion and through asking pupils to explain and explore the statements in their drafts. For example, Rachael could be asked to explain why her character *does* 'run after' Den 'all the time' (lines eight and nine), although she is well aware that it is not 'worth it' and to explore this complex, contradictory and convincing piece of human behaviour. She could relate it to things *she* does whilst knowing that they are 'not worth it'. Or she could be invited to 'let go' and really express her love, her hate or her distress. If the teacher judges that the pupil is ready to go a stage further, then questions like these on draft manuscripts are the way to reach beyond the surface of the story.

People themselves are also texts. They meet our criteria, too, being complex and as *open* as one could wish for! The following writing was done by a mixed class of third and fourth year middle school pupils working in pairs. They drew portraits of each other with the art teacher, Nanou Parmentier, and wrote 'portraits' of each other with me. Drawings and poems were published as a class magazine. The writing is planned in stages, i.e. it is an example of the second kind of drafting process in which a piece of writing is built up and edited by pupils together.

The first task was to make notes for a physical description of the partner. Close observation and attention to detail were encouraged. The second was to add notes concerning the *voice* of the subject, his or her characteristic *movements*, and examples of *behaviour* that seemed characteristic or revealing. The third was to think of comparisons (see the reference to Sandy Brownjohn's *Furniture Game* in Chapter 4) – what kind of car might your partner be like? what kind of furniture? animal? place? From all these disordered notes the portrait then had to be assembled.

Pupils were encouraged to see the portrait as a whole and choose a *theme* for it from their observations – perhaps a comparison that seemed to them an apt key to character, or an action – and to edit in relation to the theme, not necessarily using all their material but selecting according to a principle established by their choice of a unifying theme. On a small scale this is the archetypal research-and-writing process, the model of what a newspaper leader writer would have to do, or a manager in industry preparing the annual report, or a novelist. It is extraordinary that drafting edited, thematic, coherent copy from notes has not been common practice for decades in our schools, but it has not, and some junior and middle schools pupils take weeks to get used to the strange idea.

Some pupils in the 'Portraits' project class coped with the observation and comparison aspects of the task well, but did not manage to find and use a unifying theme or keynote. This was

CHARLOTTE LAWRENCE.

Her eyes are blue and her skin is white.

Under her freccdes are red blushy cheeks.

Her hair is fair. Her eyes are like studds.

Red lines hang under and over her eyes, as if she's

been sad or crying or maybe she's been staying up late.

Her nostrils are arched and she has dark pink lips.

Her heart is made of cheekiness.

She goes red when she's told to stop talking.

Her skin is soft like a touch of silk.
Her voice is determined and is sure what she is
speaking about.

by
Rachael
Lilley.

the most intellectually demanding part of the task, requiring organisation of a more sophisticated kind than the common stringing together of observations. The subject was highly motivating, however, and all the efforts have the freshness and charm of affectionate knowledge of character.

CHARLOTTE LAWRENCE

Her eyes are blue and her skin is white.
Under her freckles are red blushy cheeks.
Her hair is fair. Her eyes are like studs.
Red lines hang under and over her eyes, as if she's
been sad or crying or maybe she's been staying up late.
Her nostrils are arched and she has dark pink lips.
Her heart is made of cheekiness.
She goes red when she's told to stop talking.
Her skin is soft like a touch of silk.
Her voice is determined and is sure what she is speaking about.

Rachael Lilley (10)

DAVID

His hair is messy like a bush
His ears are small like a mouse's
His mouth is big like a cave
His nose is shiny like a mirror
His eyes are shaped like a rugby ball
His cheeks are like the Titanic (SUNK!)
His brain is full like an encyclopaedia
His body is vast like the grasslands
His arms are long like a broomstick
His legs are lanky like a tree
He is my mate called
DAVID

Garry Wiltshire (11)

MICHELLE

Michelle has freckles,
Michelle has small ears,
Blue eyes,
And blondish brown hair.
Stubby little nails,
Longish fringe,
And long neck.
Like a mouse speaking when the teacher talks.

Big nose,
Doesn't care about much,
Like if she does not finish ten SMP cards.
She speaks slang with some words like
Aint,
Neat, sometimes,
Mostly wears trousers,
But rarely skirts,
Top button open type.

Lee Baldwin (10)

Some pupils did catch on to the idea of a *key sentence* or *theme* for the portrait and edited their notes with great selectivity, producing writing which is unified in its effect. Susan uses the sense of comparison with a rabbit ingeniously (with a marvellous instinct for what is appropriate, she ends on a game of hop scotch), and Vanessa uses the theme of kindness, to which each statement relates.

LORNA MASON

A wolfing rabbit's nose
with
a little rabbit's mouth
with
little rabbit's eyes
and
a little rabbit's face.

A love for helpless
friends with asthma
(which is me!)

Loves to play hop scotch
jumping like a rabbit

A foot in each space.
Jump, hop, miss one, hop
You missed one
I did not
did
did not
did. OK.

Susan Russell (10)

Lorna Mason

A wolfing rabbits nose
with
a little rabbits mouth
with
   little rabbits eyes
and
a little rabbits face .

A love for helpless
friends with asthma
(which is me !)

Loves to play hop stotch
Jumping like a rabbit

A foot in each space .
Jump , hop , miss one , hop .
You missed one
I did not ,
did ,
did not ,
did . O.K. .

By . Susan . Russell

NATASHA EBBOTSON

Natasha's eyes are a soft blue
they look like caring eyes.
Natasha has a nice voice
that too sounds caring.
She is a great laugh to be with.
She's a person that would think about
going and ringing old ladies' doorbells
but wouldn't because it's cruel.
Natasha has a lovely smile
with lovely white teeth
and everybody likes her
and she is great to be with.

                                        Vanessa Sykes

Thought cannot subsist on a diet without nourishment; if the
imagination is fed on sub-standard scraps then it just churns like
a treadmill. These principles apply whatever form the stimulus
takes. With good texts, all pupils, not just those who are talented
poets, can practise observation and articulation, and question
the subject in a penetrating way that opens into deeper areas of
understanding. They learn to use texts for their own *thinking*.

PART THREE
The Writing Process

9 The Writers' Workshop

> Probably, indeed, the larger part of the labour of an author in composing his work is critical labour: the labour of sifting, combining, constructing, expunging, correcting, testing: this frightful toil is as much critical as creative.
>
> T. S. Eliot

I pointed out in Chapter 2 that writing is *always* a thinking process of working at the words, *often* a matter of crafting entertainments and engaging socially with others on collaborations and only *sometimes* is it 'art-making'.

The 'art-making' is what may need special conditions and an unpredictable time-scale but essentially it arises out of the circumstances of your writing; a 'good' reader; plenty of encouragement; an established sense of a craft; openness and tolerance. People are busy, some at set tasks and some on self-chosen subjects. Good ideas and good work will be welcomed with real appreciation. In this climate anyone who is inspired with an idea for a poem will not see any demarcation line between the poetry class and their own time. They will write when moved to write and bring their draft to you at the first opportunity.

The writers' workshop is an ideal place for the thinking and crafting process. It is the receiving place and it is also the craftshop where things are shaped and polished and critically considered. Most of what goes on in the workshop is not forging in the white heat of inspiration, but consolidating, sharing, reconsidering, searching for a word, planning, reading-with-a-purpose as a writer reads, and typing.

The workshop, therefore, is basically free, continuous writing punctuated by tutorials with the teacher. The aim of organising the class in this way is to create ideal working conditions – as nearly as possible the conditions of a writer working at home with a friendly adviser to consult when necessary. Pupils work as they would if they were not in a bizarre institution called school. They read and write what interests them, at their own pace, prompted and encouraged by the teacher-as-personal-tutor (as contrasted with the teacher-as-prescriber-of-wholeclass-tasks). The teacher/tutor rôle is like the rôle of a professional adviser: a literary agent, publisher's editor, or friendly co-writer.

The advantages of organising the classroom in the style of a writer's' workshop are:

1 Learning is individualised. Pupils work at a pace that suits them and at their own ability levels without feeling that they are unable to keep up with the work of the rest of the class, or that they are held back. The workshop is infinitely flexible.
2 Pupils take responsibility for choosing their own subjects and their own methods of study. Initially, the most dependent ones can find the level of responsibility burdensome, but in time they develop the maturity to benefit from it.
3 Through the emphasis on individual tutorials, pupils learn that their writing is taken seriously, that the quality can be improved by attention to detail, and that they are making progress.
4 Through the 'sharings' and the encouragement they are given to help and advise each other, pupils gain experience of learning as a collaborative venture; they discover that discussion with their friends can help them solve academic and creative problems. This is not a contradiction of what was said in 1 above; the focus is on the individual writing, but pupils learn how to bounce ideas off their colleagues.
5 Through the use of the writing journal (see the next chapter), pupils focus their attention on the meaning of their education and on recording their developing insights into personal and technical skills.
6 The writers' workshop enacts a view of writing as drafting: a continuous, developing, skilled, serious craft.

How to set up a Workshop

The workshop will need a launch-pad. It is best introduced after the playfulness of the 'Mucking about in words' phase, and after the first group poem and its follow-up poem. The planned 'writing programme' for a class has two stages: 'Getting the flow' and 'Using the flow'. 'Getting the flow' consists of 'mucking about in words', the group poem and the aids to motivation discussed in earlier chapters. 'Using the flow' is the job of the writers' workshop and its tutorial system. Until the writing starts flowing in, it is difficult to do anything at all in a workshop. Once it starts, however, each pupil will have received praise, been 'published' in one way or another and will have begun to understand the aims of the writing programme – and there will be enough momentum to carry through the first sessions of the workshop, until its nature is established.

To set up the workshop you will need to:

1 Explain the purpose of the workshop and encourage pupils to see the long-term and short-term aims of their education.
2 Establish the workshop on the time-table. With younger pupils it needs to take place at least twice a week and preferably daily, for anything up to an hour. With older pupils it can be one double period (or more) per week, set aside for GCSE coursework, for example.
3 Introduce the use of folders and journals and establish the resources you need. Everyone must know where to find more paper and materials to make display copies or to type up finished work. You need also to establish a class poetry library.
4 Start writing. If you introduce the workshop along the lines recommended above, then pupils will already be engaged in writing tasks which will launch them straight into the workshop. Discuss how to choose new topics for writing (see below).
5 Agree a motivating end-product for the term – a performance or publication of some kind.
6 Agree the ground rules. These concern showing respect for others who are working, not disturbing them, keeping the noise level within acceptable bounds. These are the obligations. There are also rights – the right to work undisturbed and the right to tutorial help, principally. Decide whether you think it is better to establish the ground rules from the start or negotiate them in response to problems as they arise.*

Writing: Teacher and Children at Work by Donald H. Graves gives a full and detailed account of how to organise a writers' workshop. Although it is mostly concerned with primary age pupils and prose rather than poetry, it is excellent on the principles of teaching writing, the environment, the tutorials, research evidence about the writing

The Writing Workshop in Operation

If you walk into a writing workshop lesson, you will see most of the pupils writing quietly. They are working on different subjects. The teacher is sitting with one pupil discussing the wording of her description. Another similar conversation is going on over the other side of the room where two pupils are discussing the ending of a new poem one of them has just finished. They are referring to notes that the teacher wrote by way of 'marking' (tutoring) the writing between lessons, but they are experienced now and make their own decisions with confidence. One pupil is absorbed in designing a magazine cover; two others are browsing in poetry books from the class library; one girl is reading D. H. Lawrence animal poems, brought in by the teacher because she is trying to write about a frog she found in her garden but has run out of ideas.

The lesson will have started without any formal introduction: the pupils know the routine. They will have come into the room, collected their folders and settled down to write. They may be interrupted by the teacher to hear someone's new work, discuss an aspect of writing which some are finding problematic, or have a new book or subject recommended to them, but most of the time they will work on their own.

There will, however, be problems with this process:

1 The development of high quality work will depend substantially upon the quality of the tutorials.
2 Some children will have difficulty coping in a mature way with the responsibility they are given and will need to adjust their attitudes. (It is possible to do very little indeed in a workshop, where what has to be done is not actually defined in terms of the number of pages.)
3 Establishing good work habits and organisational routines is vital if the workshop is to succeed.
4 You will need to devise ways of sustaining the momentum, especially for those who normally lack confidence or are inclined to be lazy, and of keeping the flow of writing coming over an extended period.
5 Record-keeping is more difficult than when all pupils work simultaneously on a common task.

---

process and record-keeping. Those who feel the need for a fuller treatment of organisational matters than I have room for here will find Graves' book very helpful.

To take these points in turn: the quality of tutoring is discussed fully in Chapter 3. Understanding aims and shifting attitudes is best addressed by explicit explanations of the workshop method, and by the use of the writer's journal (see Chapter 10). The journal is an exercise book which is used as a combination of a writer's notebook, an educational year planner, and a place to record notes on technical aspects of writing and of literature. It is a jotting book for all ideas relevant to learning through writing. It also carries three lists: a list of pieces of completed writing; a list of subjects for future writing; and a list of 'things I have learned to do'. Chapter 10 explains the important role of the journal in prising 'awareness' out of educational experiences and gives examples of its uses.

Points 4 and 5 require more detailed discussion.

Five Ways of Sustaining Momentum

The writers' workshop *could* lack variation and appear to be endless. The answer is to punctuate it with various events that mark progress and act as goals to aim at, thereby sustaining the momentum of the workshop.

The first is to keep progress and success constantly before the minds of the pupils in ways already described: by marking regularly and in an encouraging way; by the tutorials; by highlighting the context and aims of the workshop.

The second way is to introduce new themes and forms as subjects for writing. One has to be careful with this. At the 'Getting the flow' stage the teacher is feeding in the ideas to stimulate writing, but the initiative soon passes to the pupils. They will be writing on topics they have chosen for themselves, taking responsibility and appreciating the freedom of the workshop. It can annoy them, when they are already writing quietly, if you keep interrupting to introduce new 'stimuli'! The best compromise is probably to leave those alone who are engaged on something that absorbs them and introduce your new ideas to those in the class whose interest seems to be flagging and who appear to be in need of a change. (For some suggested activities, see Chapters 6, 7 and 8.)

The third way is to help pupils start a new piece of writing after the project of the moment is finished. The running list of new topics in the writing journal will provide them with starting points. Donald H. Graves makes another good suggestion in *Writing: Teachers and Children at Work*: he describes 'modelling' the process of choosing a theme or subject. I have found this works well. You share a topic-choice of your own with the class, talking about how you considered three or four ideas that appealed to you, made some notes, realised that one would be more difficult than the others, explored the scope of the topics, and decided to pursue one. The 'decision' will sometimes be a reasoned one, and sometimes something that just 'happens' as you warm to an idea. It is most effective if you can read extracts from your own journal in which you rough out ideas and try things in different ways. In the discussion that follows these disclosures, pupils become aware of the elements involved in the process of choosing and realise that there are strategies for exploring the options. If the workshop is concerned with non-fiction writing or longer narratives you can also model processes like brainstorming, making flow-charts, essay-planning and story-planning in the same way.

The fourth way to sustain momentum is to have special 'sharings' that act as motivating peaks: assembly performances; sharing writing with another class or another school; and visits to the class by prestigious people. It is important that the headteacher lends the authority of his or her office to encouraging and praising progress. Parents, governors, other teachers and members of the community can do the same and when the workshop is established it is helpful if a professional writer visits and discusses writing issues. By this time the pupils will have a vocabulary for discussing writing – from technical terms like *drafting, editing, characterisation* and *metaphor* to a knowledgeable attitude to *beginnings, endings, themes* and *form*.

The fifth way to sustain the momentum is an extension of 'sharing'. It is to agree with the class on some end-product for the work of a term, or half-term. If the workshop focuses on producing a magazine for the end of term, performing a concert, making a radio programme or videotape, entering a national writing competition, making, binding and decorating a book each, or completing two units of GCSE coursework, they will have a real and urgent purpose for writing. I shall have more to say on the subjects of publication and performance at the end of this chapter, but first let us consider the teacher's role in the workshop once the procedures are established and, in particular, the need to devise a system of record-keeping.

Record-keeping

When the workshop is in full swing and pupils are writing their own individual projects, the teacher's role changes. The teacher is no longer the 'onlie begetter' of the sonnets, epics and limericks, the initiator and inspirer; the teacher has to *serve* the writers in the workshop as a 'facilitator', consultant and general 'fixer'. Sometimes, as above, a new initiative will be introduced to a group but the role is more likely to consist of encouraging and tutoring work-in-progress; recommending appropriate reading according to what the pupil is working on; seeing that work gets an audience; organising – and rather too often *doing!* – the typing, display, photocopying, stencil-making and printing; liaising with other groups; making arrangements for performances; and, absolutely crucial in such a busy, confusing and 'free' environment, record-keeping.

Record-keeping is essential to this 'free' form of teaching as it is in 'the integrated day', but it is complicated by having no set series of tasks done by all pupils on the same date, markable out of ten, lending themselves to summary in neat columns in a register. Teachers have their own idiosyncratic preferences about keeping notes. Do whatever suits you best but do not try to record too much and find after one hectic week that you have not the energy to sustain the system. My own preferred method is to have space to make a one-sentence comment on each piece of writing, so I rule broad columns down the page, leaving boxes big enough for about 20 words. A glance at the page reveals those who have done few pieces and reading the comment reminds me of the subject, my impressions and any special issues identified. I have a narrow column set aside for marking in code technical skills which are insecure and need addressing. Some teachers like to keep a page or two for each pupil in a file and constantly update it with notes about progress. That is splendid if you can keep it up, but 'doing-the-files' is likely to seem like the sort of major task that can't be done tonight and had better wait until the weekend or half-term. . .

You can also devise your own symbols for *sharing, publication, rewrite, absence, writer's block* and any other items that are important to your records so that you can enter a lot of information in your mark-book with the minimum of fuss.

A reliable system for record-keeping (along with the effective use of frequent brief tutorials, reviewing all folders at least weekly and keeping an eye on the list of titles in the writing journals) is a key means of ensuring you are on top of the situation. Just as importantly, it will make clear to everyone that the teacher can tell the difference between pupils who are making real progress but taking it easy today by putting their feet up with an entertaining poetry book and those who habitually avoid any real engagement by reading aimlessly and pretending to be thinking about something.

Donald Graves' *Writing: Teachers and Children at Work* describes some elegantly simple record-keeping ideas focused on particular aspects of the writers' workshop: using +, − or 0 to indicate a positive, negative or neutral or indeterminate response, the teacher can quickly mark observations on a grid. The responses to tutorials can be recorded in this way, and so can pupils' responses to each other's work in 'sharings' (which will identify those who need tutoring on their social sensitivity and the art of constructive questioning). This will give a rough guide to those with positive or negative attitudes.

Publication

I argued in Chapter 3 that 'publication' of some kind (any form of presentation from display to performance) is one of the two fundamental motivating forces and I shall now consider the organisational and technical implications of publishing. For younger children, making personal, bound books is a satisfying way of gaining prestige for their work. Bindings can be prepared in advance by a team of parent-helpers, or the making of bindings can be a class craft project. Children's own decorations to the pages and to the cover will give each book a personal charm. There are two ways of binding the pages: a large sheet of paper can be folded twice (to make an eight–page book) or three times (to make a sixteen–page book) sewn along the spine with strong cotton thread and then cut into pages; or pages can be clipped together, normally with a stapler, and then attached to the back cover of the stiff binding. There are plenty of sources of information on bookbinding as a craft activity, and teachers can improvise very successfully. If the writing has gone hand-in-hand with a study of illuminated manuscripts, scrolls, early printing, or Japanese calligraphy (to go with haiku) then the books can be adapted to the special character of the project.

With older classes (from 10 up) magazines are the best way to publish. A magazine is a group production which proves that all take part. It reaches a wider audience than a single book and has more impact on parents and the local community. Children often like to sell copies for charity. There is quite a lot of tedious preparatory work involved in publishing a magazine, and not everything can be delegated to pupils – if they did it all it would take weeks and become burdensome.

With a poetry magazine it is not a good idea to democratise the editorial process completely and hand control to elected editors – you may end up with pages of jokes, pop-star rankings and cartoons, with very little poetry, or find that the editors interpret their task as *selecting* poems, which of course involves *rejecting* the writing of some unfortunate classmate. Keep control of the selection process yourself, seeing that every pupil in the class is represented by a piece of writing and that the magazine is kept to manageable proportions. What the pupil-editors can do is take responsibility for the design and layout, for as much of the stencil-cutting, typing or photocopying as they can cope with, and for decisions about the title, cover design, charity, print run, complimentary copies, and advertising and distribution.

There is no doubt that the technology of school publishing gets better all the time. The new generation of photocopiers – that reverse and copy both sides automatically and sort and collate pages – will take all the hard work out of magazine production, but at the moment they cost too much for most schools. Full colour photocopiers are marvellous but are not going to be cheap enough to be practical in the foreseeable future. Word-processing and desk-top publishing linked to a good printer will take care of the proof-reading, retyping, and paste-up stages of editing. They will bring other benefits too: they will make it easier to draft long texts, and they are very well suited to collaborative decision-making, with a group clustered around the keyboard arguing about *which is the very best phrase for the purpose.*

Any comments on the technology of magazine production will soon be out of date and you will all have access through your Teachers Resource Centre or local college to different kinds of reprographic machinery, so I shall keep my comments very brief and general. Ink duplicating gives a better appearance than spirit, and both are cheaper at the moment than photocopying, but photocopying is closing the gap and will clearly replace these forms of printing soon because it is so much more convenient, flexible and smart in appearance (and clean to operate!).

For the cover of a poetry magazine, stiff card with good artwork is more appropriate than the kind of newspaper format produced by desk-top publishing programs.

The simplest way to bind pages is with a heavy-duty stapler. The collation and binding of pages are operations that can be done in class. Sheer numbers help here: 30 pupils can make copies 30 times faster than one teacher can. Also, they feel that they have 'made' the magazine. In a half-hour lesson you can collate and staple a complete run of 100 or so copies.

The other operations – typing (if you choose to use it), stencil-cutting, and printing – *can* be done in class by the pupils, but are difficult to organise efficiently when you have 30 pupils to cope with and they also interrupt the writing. These activities can be done at lunch-time by an enthusiastic editorial board of pupils, but very often the bulk of the work falls to the teacher. You will need to get some help. School secretaries, resources technicians, parent-helpers and business studies departments can all be pressed into service.

A magazine made on a duplicator only costs the price of a ream or two of paper, but if you photocopy it, it will cost a few pence a sheet or a little more. If you plan in advance you may be able to raise the money by asking for sponsorship from local businesses. The Co-op has Education Officers who are sometimes willing to support special educational projects and other large business concerns have a budget allocation for worthy causes – but you may have to catch them at the right time of the year, before all the budget is committed.

Performance

The other form of 'publication' is public performance. This has the serious purpose of completing the communication-circle which makes writing worthwhile: writer to audience, audience feedback to writer. There are other benefits too, but the main point of performance is to have fun.

We have a cultural tradition of listening to songs, and currently there are rappers, dub poets and pop poets who hold large audiences with recitals of rhythmic, rhymed verse narratives. The ancient traditions were of lyric singers and epic bards, but epic bards have not been much in evidence for hundreds of years and their role passed to balladeers, then novelists, and now television producers. There never was much of a public for *spoken* short lyrics. We have generally consumed short poems by reading from the page. Some short poems can be successfully read aloud, however, particularly the light and humorous ones, but many release their flavour only on a second reading and do not work well in an auditorium.

A programme of poetry reading must make special efforts to reach the audience if it is not to become an embarrassing event that parents sit through politely out of a sense of duty. The purpose of the exercise – entertainment – will have been subverted if the audience is bored and forced to be hypocritically indulgent, so the quality of performance is important. It must surprise listeners, entertain them, convert them and send them out saying 'I didn't expect to enjoy that, but . . .'

It is not sufficient that your pupils have written good poems, they must also dramatise them effectively. They must please both the ear and the eye. The first virtue of performance is clarity. It must look clear as well as sound clear. The creative work of preparing a group dramatisation of a poem or song, or a way of presenting it chorally, can be left to the pupils, with the teacher making the minimum of suggestions. But getting what they do to 'look clear' will be the concern of the teacher in the last stages of preparation, the pre-performance rehearsals.

First, make sure that you have a couple of sure-fire hits in the programme, one near the beginning and one to end on. If the class has not produced any comic or moving poems that are suitable, then do a full-scale production number on an already published poem that lends itself as a score for performance: Michael Rosen's 'Washing Up', complete with water-squirting washing-up liquid bottles; Edwin Morgan's 'The First Men on Mercury'; one of Edward Kamau Brathwaite's Caribbean character portraits, or an evocation of community life from 'Sun Poem' complete with mime and music; Roger McGough's 'The Lesson'; a humorous dance drama to 'Jabberwocky' by Lewis Carroll; or any one of many possible performance pieces. Vary the programme: a quiet contemplative poem contrasted with one

that 'troubles the heart'; your one choral-speaking number
contrasted with one using a single, unaccompanied voice.

Once pupils have an idea of the range of inventive possibilities
open to them (acting, mime, representing in formalised
movement, dance, adding sound effects, the range of music from
simple percussion to fully arranged scores, props and 'stage
business', lighting if available, costume, make-up), they can be
safely left to 'realise' the poetic texts. The teacher must not
control the whole process or the fun will be organised out of the
class. The teacher's role is to discourage the madly over-
complicated and impractical ideas and to help groups to clarify
the visual presentation of their best ideas and bring out contrasts
of pace, pitch and movement.

There will also need to be some class discussion about the
speaking of verse. The main point I always find myself making
is that the pace for reading a serious poem is a *quarter* the speed
of pupils' usual speech. If the words are good they must be given
some breathing space and room to resonate. Reading slowly will
not 'feel' natural to young people, so you need to give direction
and reassurance, explaining that the art of verse speaking is a
convention not quite like conversational speech.

One or two pupils will be very poor at self-presentation, and
stand – and speak – with all the panache of a snail. Use your
judgement about whether a bit of coaching and encouragement
would help or would drive them back into their shells. Pupils
will be able to work around the presentational talents of those at
their disposal; they will have a ready appreciation of who is good
at what, sort themselves out pretty effectively and will often, by
the sheer momentum of their energy, sweep a shy friend along
into an unaccustomed performing role.

Useful tools in the 'drafting' of performances are tape and
video recordings. They allow a group to see or hear what the
audience will receive. They can then work towards improving
what they recognise as problem elements. Try to tape the finished
performance – pupils will want to see it again and show it to
others.

There are several benefits to be derived from the fun of the
performance project: it makes a class into a social group –
afterwards everyone has shared an *experience* and somehow grown
together; pupils read other poems afterwards with a better sense
of sound and of how to make them communicate effectively;
they have got to know their poems inside out; they have taken

part in a creative activity that is quite complicated and involves problem-solving, joint decision-making, constructive criticism and developing communication skills, i.e. they will have been practising 'personal transferable' communication and team-working skills.

With a bit of luck they will also receive a warm response from their audience, and experience pride and satisfaction in their work. As the admirable Michael Baldwin said, 'Poetry in itself is not important, but the enjoyment of poetry is.'

10 The Writing Journal

20	Reading maketh a full man,
21	conference a readey man and
22	writing an exacte man.
23	

Francis Bacon

Writing is more exploratory than it is creative. The writer does not 'make' meaning by the use of 'imagination', though imagination comes into it. The writer digs meaning out, quarrying stones and shaping them for display or use, prising out fossil memories, collecting shells, bones and fool's gold. This requires not so much a meaning-manufacturing ability as a heightened sense of the potential meaning in things, an aptitude for drawing attention to meanings, and it is done by digging, prising, collecting and displaying – exactly the metaphors evident in Margaret Donaldson's term 'disembedding'. Writing, by its nature, is a 'disembedding' thinking activity.

STUPID

Why do I have to
   ESCAPE
from
you
her
the world
I'm weak
dumb
stupid
I can't be or I could not write this
   but
the world
wants more

Tony Nelson (16)

Tony had been painfully aware that he was not a success in school and would only gain minimal CSE qualifications, yet was sure that what he was doing was *thinking* and that his writing was evidence of this. 'The world wants more' is an eloquent distillation of that sense of humiliation we feel as we try to measure up to others' ideals and the demands of institutionalised education. For Tony, in a confusing adolescent world, writing was a way in which he could keep things still long enough to get a hold on them.

MY WORLD

I stand, and tap the crinkles from my trousers
        and watch
something had caught my attention

The corn whispered behind my back
as the shadows from the branches
above my alert head, quivered
and made a dark jigsaw
        on the patchwork grass.

I felt a tremble on my scalp
as the summer breeze crumpled and distorted
        my newly combed hair

Now I recognise the object that had
interrupted my fantasy as a curlew.
It screamed and watched me suspiciously
        whilst soaring by.

I had felt so happy here,
but soon it will be autumn
it is only right to return to the city
and leave my somewhat
        uncivilised ground.

                                        Beverley Peel (14)

Beverley transforms an ordinary enough experience into a meditation that seems to look with sad wisdom at a whole life of divided values stretching out before her. By the time the last extraordinary phrase is reached a rich and complex meaning becomes available to it. She has taken the tension between the life of pressed trousers, combed hair and the city, and the life of the dark jigsaw on the patchwork grass, and framed it within a title and conclusion that create a critical perspective. She has

attuned to her perceptions, attended to them until they come
clear, and described them.

Through poetry writing, perceptions are disembedded from
life and given meaning. Through writing in the journal, learning
is disembedded from the act of writing and from educational
experiences and given meaning. In this chapter we will consider
the uses of the journal in relation to awareness about writing,
awareness about learning, awareness about criticism, and awareness of personal responsibilities.

The Journal

The journal is a little book – memo book, exercise book, diary
or, for older pupils, perhaps a large Challenge notebook. It is
used liked a writer's Filofax, for notes, lists, drafts, and as an
educational year planner. First, it is a writer's notebook in which
to store observations for use in future poems, character sketches,
images and phrases, and in which to draft lines and plan pieces
of writing. It is also for reflections upon writing: the teacher
poses questions about aspects of the craft and pupils record their
perceptions. Secondly, the journal is used to draw attention to
the context of the learning and to enable pupils to reach an
awareness of their educational aims, to take control of their
education and plan. Thirdly, it is used for relating writing to
critical issues and practising literary criticism. Fourthly, it can
be used to facilitate communication between teacher and pupil
(and parent) through dialogues.

The teacher cannot merely issue or describe the journal and
leave it at that, however, or it will fall into disuse. The teacher
has to refer to the journal regularly, make it clear it is a central
part of the poetry writing process and set specific questions to
be addressed in the journal in order to help pupils understand
its scope and usefulness. When the habit of journal-keeping is
established, pupils will use it in their own ways. You might think
confidentiality and non-judgemental responses would be essential
for such a personal document as a journal, but in fact it does no
harm to make it assessable (at GCSE level, for example). To do
so asserts that the journal is important in a way that no amount
of exhortation can and lends it a special identity of its own in
which quality of insight and presentation are valued.

Ensure that three pages are set aside for lists. The first is a list of subjects for future pieces of writing. This helps bridge the gap between one project and the next, which is often a slack period of uncertainty and indecision. The second is a list of 'Things I have learned to do', which records the writer's increasing control of skills, from punctuation and spelling to mastery of genre-specific features like paragraphing and exposition, or the use of imagery. The third is a list of the titles of pieces of writing which have been completed and are collected in a folder – a contents page. This enables the pupil and the teacher to see at a glance the range and number of items, and to take an overview of the progress made.

Writing about Writing

Below, pupils record their learning about aspects of writing. Some comments are responses to questions posed by the teacher.

A word of warning, though: pupils will not at first be used to the kind of disembedded thinking required by the journal and you may not find the booklets packed with brilliant insights. A good deal of the note-making will be at a descriptive level, only occasionally analytical, and the insights will not be fully realised, like ten year old Reshma's:

Our group is in a muddle because we were all arguing so Mrs Wharton helped us out. Mrs Wharton told us what to do and our play was coming out right. Because everybody wanted to do each other's job we were spending most of the time on our play [*here she is giving an analytical reason*]. It was funny . . . I enjoyed doing our play. We showed our play to Mr Marsh he told us that it was a good play. Quite a few people said some comments.

A significant advance in awareness may not seem very stunning to you, the teacher, though it does represent successful use of the journal.

I have trouble with stories because I try things that are too ambitious for me to cope with.

Tanya Bell (12)

What I have learned about choosing a subject . . . I think it helps by talking about and remembering stories you already know.

When I am advised to change something I have written . . . I think I

am a failure and try again. It usually is better when I do it the
second time.

Sarah Cook (11)

What I feel when I have to sit down and write . . . I enjoy a free
subject – writing stories or poems. I enjoy free subjects better
than set subjects because you can put any idea in and use as much
imagination as you like.

Zoe Pettinger (12)

Endings I usually have trouble with because I like writing long
stories and when someone tells me to finish off I'm usually half
way through it. In other words I need more time to write a *good*
story!

Martin Davis (11)

I would like my poems to be about happiness and joyfulness

Zoe Dall (12)

All these comments represent increasing awareness about the
writing process or personal aims and are improvements on the
view that may prevail at the beginning: 'I've got it wrong and
have to do it again.' Sometimes a really gratifying aspect of
learning is recorded.

Things that look boring aren't just boring you can turn them into
what you like just look closely at your subject.

Things that you write don't have to rhyme just think what you
want to write and write it.

David Amies (12)

Learning about Learning

Pupils will become aware of the purposes for which one writes,
aware of the way writing opens up an audience for them and is
a rewarding way of sharing their perceptions. They will gain
awareness of all the elements of writing (beginnings, endings,
images, rhythms, directness of language, etc.), and of their own
individual strengths and weaknesses.

To start the class thinking, the simplest questions are best.
'What do I want to learn?' will bring a lot of contradictory
feelings about schooling into the open and if you give sufficient
discussion time, pupils will progress from purely vocational views

of education as functional to philosophical notions such as fulfilment, awareness, knowledge, understanding and skill.

Pupils should occasionally be required to plan their learning aims over a particular period, to reflect on the progress they have made over past months and pick out the significant moments of learning, the 'leaps forward' or proudest achievements. They should identify their weaknesses and set themselves targets. They should see their development over time as something with a sense of direction and a personal pattern. Each piece of writing in the journal builds on past experience of writing and leads, through the mastery of skills and the development of understanding, to a vision of oneself as a competent, articulate person. Such skills as learning to control speech punctuation, learning to write in another character's imagined voice, of learning to focus the writing on a theme and build it consciously towards a conclusion are significant milestones and should be celebrated as such. Draw attention to these matters and ask pupils to articulate their sense of progress in their journals.

As far as study skills are concerned, pupils can learn to see the significance of their idiosyncratic ways of concentrating, of using the resources available (pen and paper, books, teacher, peers, computer), of finding a theme, of pacing themselves, of reacting to criticism, of coping with difficulties, of extending themselves into more ambitious writing, and so on. The teacher once again has to raise the issues by asking questions and organising group discussion followed by note-making in journals. Journals can also be used to encourage particular study techniques, like brainstorming, making flow-diagrams and paragraph planning.

It is much more valuable to complete one good piece of sustained writing, from planning, through drafting, to evaluating, to be aware of how the skills involved are important to your life as a learner and to gain a sense of the meaning of writing as a human activity, than to write twelve routine pieces of marking-fodder for the insatiable teacher. Research evidence from a recent APU (Assessment of Performance Unit) study and from surveys conducted by participants in the SCDC National Writing Project, shows that pupils' own views of quality in writing are superficial and almost entirely focused on spelling and neatness. They must have derived their scale of values from their school environment.

In *Assessment of Writing, Pupils Aged 11 and 15*, Janet White of the APU comments, 'The APU evidence could be interpreted as suggesting that emphasis should not be placed on "skills" in isolation, but on the concept of writing as something which has a place and purpose in communicative systems, and a personal value for the pupil concerned. In such an approach, questions of "correctness" arise as a by-product of successful communication, rather than forming the staple of language work.'

Critical Awareness

Critical thinking is developed through evaluating your own writing. As we have seen, a completed poem is a free-standing entity which takes on a life of its own. You can stand back from it and see yourself from the outside. One of the most important functions of the teacher is training pupils to be their own critical audience. When pupils are able to help each other, it not only cuts the teacher's workload, it makes criticism *immediately useful* (think of the millions of hours expended on Shakespeare and Milton each year to no apparent purpose!) and it draws *generosity* into criticism. You might fear that children would be brutal and damaging to their peers but that is not the experience of teachers who have taken the risk. On the contrary, the young are conscious of the danger of hurting each other's feelings and practise criticism with great tact and kindness. If anyone does use it as an opportunity to hurt another, then the teacher will need to address the issue and sort it out, but, I repeat, it is very rare indeed.

Criticism should be structured by the teacher initially, who sets as a class activity one day the task of reviewing writing in pairs and offers questions to guide the criticism, such as: 'Is anything unclear to you?' 'Is the ending overcooked?' 'Is every phrase in a consistent style?' 'Could it be cut, and would a little editing improve it?'

The journal can also be used for self-criticism. It is this kind of question that pupils will come to apply to their own writing, reflecting on where they have succeeded and where they have failed.

At the level of genre awareness, pupils can come to understand how their writing takes its place in a tradition of lyric poetry, narrative, or criticism, and makes use of conventions of address and techniques specific to the genre. For example, in the course of writing long stories, pupils should be asked to comment briefly in their journals on the special problems of *beginnings* – an arresting opening, introducing characters, exposition, scene setting, establishing the narrative point of view, maintaining page-turning suspense, and how they identify whether the story will be a romance, an adventure or a horror story from the first sentences. When writing songs, take a little time to record findings in the journal:

> I can make up songs in my head if I stamp my feet and shout the words (in my imagination).
>
> Sumita (10)

The journal also becomes a record of responses to reading. As well as reviews, character sketches, 'extensions' and analysis, it can also include ideas drawn from books, television programmes, films or pop songs, which are either intriguing in themselves or are noted because they are going to be used in a piece of writing in the future. Pupils can also collect quotations from writers about the skills of writing and the demands of particular genres.

Dialogues

The journal can also be used as a way of holding a dialogue with the teacher. Angela (10) is quoted in *About Writing No. 2* (1986), the SCDC National Writing Project newsletter, as holding the following dialogue with her teacher:

> I think you will get cross because I lose my things and get tomato all over a library book. I'm sorry I get so worried all the time.
>
> If things are an accident I really don't and won't get cross. DON'T WORRY, OK!
>
> OK and that's a deal a DEAL!

There is no reason why parents should not also join in, as long as the dialogues do not become too popular and time-consuming! The value of communicating directly with the family about study is inestimable.

In the cases of those few dependent pupils who mistake the freedom of the workshop for Liberty Hall, cannot accept the responsibility in a mature way and exploit the situation to avoid working, a sustained dialogue will be required in which the teacher spells out (again and again!) what the purposes, opportunities and rules of the workshop are. The teacher maintains a balance between being very encouraging and refusing to accept the responsibility for all the pupil's decisions. If parents can be encouraged to take their part too in encouraging the child to be more independent and to take responsibility for decisions then progress is much more rapid.

It is because the journal creates the space and the means for reflections of the kind discussed in this chapter that the teacher can use it, over a period of time, to help the pupils to see the direction of their learning, and to enable a reorientation of their attitudes to take place. The pupils' own responsibility for their choices and their futures is placed constantly before their eyes. With highly dependent personalities it is a long and wearisome business, but that observation will not come as a surprise to experienced teachers. The rewards are great: your pupils become more conscious of the value of their education, develop a remarkable maturity of judgement, and become co-operative and constructive critics of each other's progress in a community enthusiastically dedicated to the craft of writing.

Bibliography and Further Reading

There is a useful booklist of poetry books for children, with comments, arranged by age range, called *Poetry for Children: a 'Signal' Bookguide* edited by Jill Bennett and Adrian Chambers and published by The Thimble Press (1984). It is available from the National Book League, Book House, 45 East Hill, London SW18 2QZ.

Children as Writers, Award-winning entries in the W. H. Smith Children's Literary Competition was published annually by Heinemann Educational until recently, and now by Macmillan. Tabitha Tuckett's poem on p. 127 is from the 1983 edition.

Teachers and Writers magazine is available from 84 Fifth Avenue, New York 10011.

AUDEN, W. H. (1958) *W. H. Auden: a selection by the author*. London: Faber and Faber Ltd. (Also available in Penguin.)

BALDWIN, MICHAEL (1959) *Poetry Without Tears*. London: Routledge and Kegan Paul.

BALDWIN, MICHAEL (1963) *Billy the Kid: an anthology of tough verse*. London: Hutchinson Educational.

BENTON, MICHAEL and PETER (1975) *Poetry Workshop*. Sevenoaks: Hodder and Stoughton.

BENTON, PETER (1986) *Pupil, Teacher, Poem*. Sevenoaks Hodder and Stoughton.

BERRY, JAMES (1981) *Bluefoot Traveller*. London: Harrap.

BLYTH, R. H. (1949–52) *Haiku*, in four volumes. Tokyo: The Hokuseido Press.

BROWN, STEWART (ed.) (1984) *Caribbean Poetry Now*. Sevenoaks: Hodder and Stoughton

BROWNJOHN, SANDY (1980) *Does It Have To Rhyme?* Sevenoaks: Hodder & Stoughton.

BROWNJOHN, SANDY (1982) *What Rhymes With Secret?* Sevenoaks: Hodder & Stoughton.

BROWNJOHN, SANDY and ALAN (1985) *Meet and Write: a teaching anthology of contemporary poetry*, Volumes 1, 2 and 3. Sevenoaks: Hodder & Stoughton.

166   TEACHING THROUGH POETRY

BROWNJOHN, SANDY and WHITAKER, JANET (1985) *Word Games* and *More Word Games*. Sevenoaks: Hodder & Stoughton.

BURNETT, PAULA (ed.) (1986) *The Penguin Book of Caribbean Verse*. Harmondsworth: Penguin.

CAUSLEY, CHARLES (ed.) *The Batsford Book of Stories in Verse for Children*. London: Batsford.

CAUSLEY, CHARLES (ed.) *The Puffin Book of Magic Verse*. Harmondsworth: Penguin.

CAUSLEY, CHARLES (ed.) (1978) *The Puffin Book of Salt-Sea Verse*. Harmondsworth: Penguin.

COLLINS, MAL et al. (ed.) (1977) *The Big Red Songbook*. London: The Pluto Press.

COPE, WENDY (1986) *Making Cocoa for Kingsley Amis*. London: Faber and Faber Ltd.

CORBETT, PIE and MOSES, BRIAN (1986) *Catapults and Kingfishers: Teaching Poetry in Primary Schools*. Oxford: Oxford University Press.

DES (1978) *Primary Education in England*. London: HMSO.

DES (1983) *9–13 Middle Schools: an illustrative survey*. London: HMSO.

DES (1987a) *A Survey of the Teaching of A Level English Literature in 20 Mixed Sixth Forms in Comprehensive Schools*. London: HMSO.

DES (1987b) *Teaching Poetry in the Secondary School: An HMI View*. London: HMSO.

DEUTSCH, ANDRE and SAVILL, MERVYN (eds) (1946) *Villon Ballades*. London: Alan Wingate.

DONALDSON, MARGARET (1978) *Children's Minds*. London: Fontana.

EDWARDS, G. and HAYES, F. (1978) *Into English Six*. Huddersfield: Schofield and Sims.

EGAN, DESMOND and HARTNETT, MICHAEL (eds) (1978) *Choice*. Dublin: Goldsmith Press.

ELIOT, T. S. (1974) *The Illustrated Old Possum: Old Possum's Book of Practical Cats*. London: Faber and Faber Ltd.

EWART, GAVIN (1985) *The Young Pobble's Guide to his Toes*. London: Hutchinson.

FERLINGHETTI, LAWRENCE (trans.) *Jacques Prévert: Paroles*. San Francisco: City Lights Books.

FINNEGAN, RUTH (ed.) (1982) *The Penguin Book of Oral Poetry*. Harmondsworth: Penguin.

FITZGERALD, ROBERT (trans.) (1975) *Homer The Iliad*. Bognor Regis: Anchor Publications.

FRANKL, VICTOR E. (1970) *Psychotherapy and Existentialism: selected papers on Logotherapy*. London: Souvenir Press. (Also available in Pelican Books.)

GRAVES, DONALD H. (1983) *Writing: Teachers and Children at Work*. London: Heinemann Educational.

HEANEY, SEAMUS and HUGHES, TED (eds) (1982) *The Rattle Bag*. London: Faber and Faber Ltd.

HUGHES, TED (1976) *Season Songs*. London: Faber and Faber Ltd.

HUGHES, TED (1981) *Under the North Star*. London: Faber and Faber Ltd.

HUGHES, TED (1986) *Flowers and Insects*. London: Faber and Faber Ltd.

ILEA (1982) *City Lines: Poems by London School Students*. London: ILEA English Centre.

ILEA RESEARCH AND STATISTICS BRANCH (1986) *ILEA Junior School Project*.

Available from Information Section, Addington Street Annexe, County Hall, SE1 7UY.

KEYNES, GEOFFREY (ed.) (1966) *William Blake: Complete Writings*. Oxford: Oxford University Press.

KOCH, KENNETH (1974) *Rose, Where Did You Get That Red?* New York: Vintage Books.

KOCH, KENNETH (1980) *Wishes, Lies and Dreams*. London: Harper and Row.

LAING, R. D. (1970) *Knots*. Harmondsworth: Penguin.

LEAVIS, F. R. (1943) *Education and the University*. London: Chatto and Windus.

LIPMAN, MATTHEW, SHARP, ANN MARGARET and OSCANYAN, FREDERICK S. (1980) *Philosophy in the Classroom*. Philadelphia: Temple University Press/The Institute for the Advancement of Philosophy for Children (IAPC). Director Matthew Lipman is based at Montclair State College; when corresponding with regard to book or journal orders write to First Mountain Foundation, Box 196, Montclair, New Jersey 07042.

MANSFIELD, ROGER and ARMSTRONG, ISOBEL (eds) (1976) *A Sudden Line*. Oxford: Oxford University Press.

MCGOUGH, ROGER and ROSEN, MICHAEL (1979) *You Tell Me*. London: Viking Kestrel.

NAB/UGC (1984) 'A joint statement by the University Grants Committee and the National Advisory Body for Local Authority Higher Education' published simultaneously in *A Strategy for Higher Education in the Late 1980s and Beyond* (NAB) and *A Strategy for Higher Education into the 1990s* (UGC).

NICHOLLS, JUDITH (1987) *Midnight Forest*. London: Faber and Faber Ltd.

O'LOCHLAINN, COLM (ed.) (1978) *Irish Street Ballads* and *More Irish Street Ballads*. London: Pan Books.

OPIE, IONA and PETER (1959) *The Lore and Language of Schoolchildren*. Oxford: Oxford University Press.

ORME, DAVID and SALE, JAMES (1987) *The Poetry Show*. Volumes 1 and 2 (3 in press). Basingstoke: Macmillan Education.

PALMER, ROY (1973) *The Valiant Sailor*. Cambridge: Cambridge University Press.

PALMER, ROY (1973) *The Painful Plough*. Cambridge: Cambridge University Press.

PALMER, ROY (1974) *A Touch on the Times: Songs of Social Change 1770–1914*. Harmondsworth: Penguin Educational.

REEVES, JAMES (1978) *Arcadian Ballads*. London: Heinemann Educational.

RIFFATERRE, MICHAEL (1978) *The Semiotics of Poetry*. London: Methuen University Paperbacks.

SCDC (Schools Curriculum Development Committee) (1986) *About Writing, SCDC Newsletter*. SCDC Publications, available from The National Writing Project, Newcombe House, 45 Notting Hill Gate, London W11 3JB.

SKELTON, ROBIN (1971) *The Practice of Poetry*. London: Heinemann.

STILLMAN, FRANCES (1966) *The Poet's Manual and Rhyming Dictionary*. London: Thames and Hudson Ltd.

STONE, BRIAN (trans.) (1964) *Mediaeval English Verse*. Harmondsworth: Penguin.

STRYK, LUCIEN and IKEMOTO, TAKASHI (1981) *The Penguin Book of Zen Poetry*. Harmondsworth: Penguin.

SUMMERFIELD, GEOFFREY (ed.) (1968) *Voices* and *Junior Voices*. Harmondsworth: Penguin.

THORNTON, R. K. R. (ed.) (1970) *Poetry of the Nineties*. Harmondsworth: Penguin.

WALSH, MARCUS (ed.) (1979) *Selected Poems – Christopher Smart*. Manchester: Carcanet.

WATTS, ALAN W. (1957) *The Way of Zen*. London: Thames and Hudson Ltd. (Also available in Pelican Books.)

WHITE, J. (1986) *Assessment of Writing, Pupils Aged 11 and 15*. Windsor: NFER/Nelson for the APU (Assessment of Performance Unit).

WILLIAMS, EMMETT (ed.) (1967) *Anthology of Concrete Poetry*. New York: Something Else Press.

WILLIAMS, WILLIAM CARLOS (1968) *Selected Poems of William Carlos Williams*. New York: New Directions.

WITKIN, ROBERT (1974) *The Intelligence of Feeling*. London: Heinemann Educational.

ZARANKA, WILLIAM (ed.) (1984) *Brand X Poetry: a Parody Anthology*. London: Picador.

ZAVATSKY, BILL and PADGETT, RON (1977) *The Whole Word Catalogue 2*. New York: Teachers and Writers Collaborative/McGraw Hill.